Elements in the Renaissance
edited by
John Henderson
Birkbeck, University of London, and Wolfson College, University of Cambridge
Jonathan K. Nelson
Syracuse University Florence

MAKING NEWS IN RENAISSANCE EUROPE

Brendan Dooley
University College Cork

Shaftesbury Road, Cambridge CB2 8EA, United Kingdom

One Liberty Plaza, 20th Floor, New York, NY 10006, USA

477 Williamstown Road, Port Melbourne, VIC 3207, Australia

314–321, 3rd Floor, Plot 3, Splendor Forum, Jasola District Centre,
New Delhi – 110025, India

Cambridge University Press is part of Cambridge University Press & Assessment,
a department of the University of Cambridge.

We share the University's mission to contribute to society through the pursuit of
education, learning and research at the highest international levels of excellence.

www.cambridge.org
Information on this title: www.cambridge.org/9781009571791

DOI: 10.1017/9781009358835

© Brendan Dooley 2026

This publication is in copyright. Subject to statutory exception and to the provisions
of relevant collective licensing agreements, no reproduction of any part may take
place without the written permission of Cambridge University Press & Assessment.

When citing this work, please include a reference to the DOI 10.1017/9781009358835

First published 2026

A catalogue record for this publication is available from the British Library

*A Cataloging-in-Publication data record for this Element is available from the Library
of Congress*

ISBN 978-1-009-57179-1 Hardback
ISBN 978-1-009-35881-1 Paperback
ISSN 2631-9101 (online)
ISSN 2631-9098 (print)

Cambridge University Press & Assessment has no responsibility for the persistence
or accuracy of URLs for external or third-party internet websites referred to in this
publication and does not guarantee that any content on such websites is, or will remain,
accurate or appropriate.

For EU product safety concerns, contact us at Calle de José Abascal, 56, 1°, 28003
Madrid, Spain, or email eugpsr@cambridge.org

Making News in Renaissance Europe

Elements in the Renaissance

DOI: 10.1017/9781009358835
First published online: March 2026

Brendan Dooley
University College Cork
Author for correspondence: Brendan Dooley, b.dooley@ucc.ie

Abstract: The regular public transmission of news was one of the great inventions of the Renaissance. This Element, while offering a general account of news in the period, will convey the latest research results concerning the dynamics and significance of this major development. Drivers of change, apart from sheer curiosity, included state officials seeking opportunities, merchants seeking markets, writers seeking jobs. Traditional oral settings for news exchange, in homes, at court, and in public squares, from this period onward would have a constant supply of new topics of conversation originating not only from local occurrences but from far away, and not only from books, pamphlets and private letters, but also from regularly produced news sheets – first handwritten, then printed –covering what were thought to be the major events of the day, with significant effects on widespread ways of thinking and behaving.

This Element also has a video abstract:
www.cambridge.org/EREN_Dooley_abstract

Keywords: media storms, news coverage, news values, journalistic gatekeeping, police use of force

© Brendan Dooley 2026

ISBNs: 9781009571791 (HB), 9781009358811 (PB), 9781009358835 (OC)
ISSNs: 2631-9101 (online), 2631-9098 (print)

Contents

Introduction   1

1 What's News?   5

2 News in the Mail   12

3 Dawn of the Newsletter   24

4 News in Print   46

    Conclusion   67

    References   71

Introduction

"Hispaniola is a miracle: the mountains and the hills and the plains, and the pastures, and the lands so beautiful and fertile ... The harbors are beyond belief, and the rivers are many and great, mostly containing gold ... There are many spices and great mines of gold and other metals."

Such was the report that began to circulate among European readers and listeners from April of 1493, first penned as a letter by Christopher Columbus to the Spanish court (Ramos Perez 1983).[1] What the initial reaction may have been to some of the most remarkable news ever distributed up to that time can easily be imagined. Apart from the astonishment of individuals wherever there was access to the many manuscript or printed copies, cash-starved regimes throughout Europe stood at attention. The fanciful geography, at first limited to existing continents, only added to the sense of wonder. As often was the case of the most surprising reports, the reality of the New World took a while to sink in, and not before a good deal more observing and reporting had taken place.

Innovation was the order of the day, and geographical knowledge was only one of many areas where major changes were under way. And to the period's well-known contributions in literature and the arts, we must add yet another, less widely recognized. For just when the Columbus story broke, much was going on in the world of the news media of the time (let's call them that), with long-term repercussions still being felt today, in terms of who knows what and when do they know it. The one major earthshaking outcome we will be discussing in this Element is the Renaissance invention of the regular weekly transmission of news.

From the late fifteenth century onward, specially designed writings bearing the news of the day circulated along the main public mail routes, increasing exponentially in number and volume as these routes covered more and more territory. The Columbus letter was a one-off, an occasional piece, as were the printed versions derived from it (Figure 1). Already beginning to circulate regularly at the time were sheets belonging to a new genre of handwritten newsletters, which soon began to assume a key role and would eventually form the basis, a century later, for the first printed newspapers. Such were the ancestors, give or take a few technological developments in between, of modern daily news.

Preconditions for all this, of course, were the appropriate means of transport and networks of transmission to carry the news. But those were evolving rapidly in our period. Already in the early Renaissance the busiest international merchant companies relied on sophisticated systems of private connections in order

---

[1] Translations are by the present writer except where indicated.

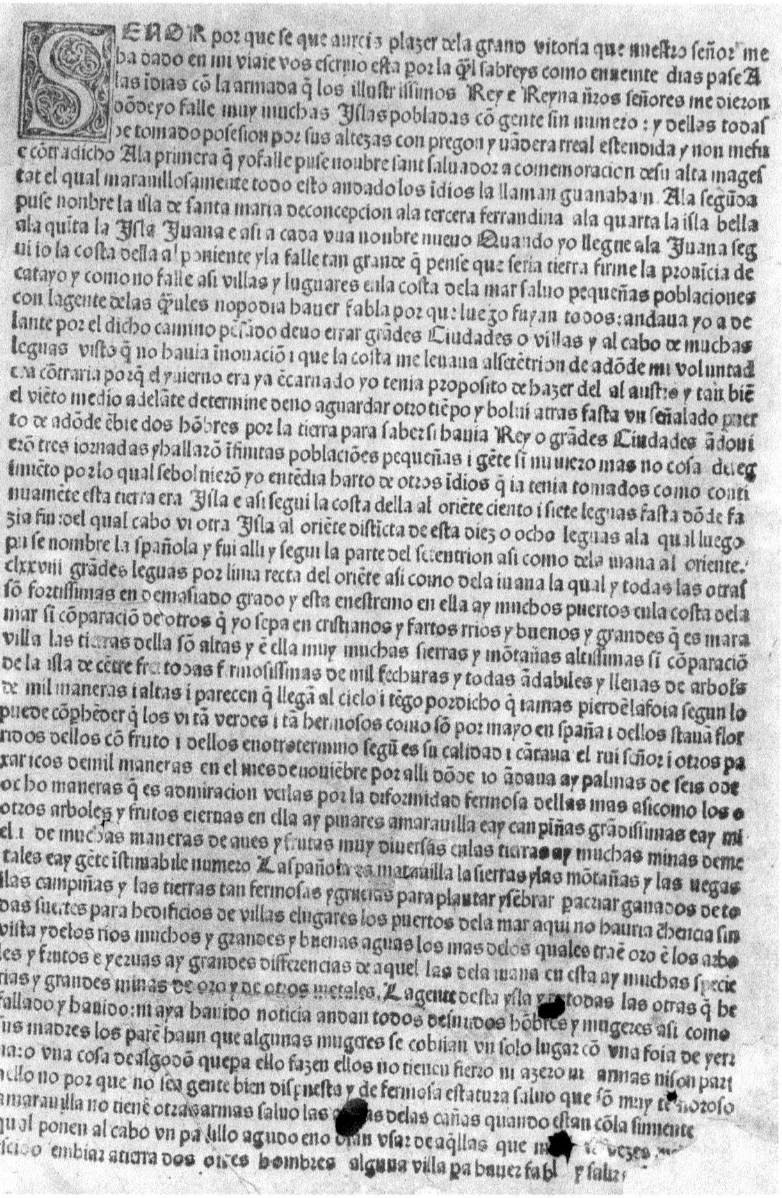
SEÑOR por que se que aureis plazer dela grand vitoria que nuestro señor me
ha dado en mi viaie vos escrivo esta por la ql sabreys como en xxxiii dias pase A
las idias cō la armada q̄ los illustrissimos Rey e Reyna nros señores me dieron
dōde yo falle muy muchas Yslas pobladas cō gente sin numero : y dellas todas
he tomado posesion por sus altezas con pregon y vādera rreal estendida y non mefu
e cōtradicho Ala primera q̄ yo falle puse nonbre sant saluador a comemoracion desu alta mages
tat el qual maravillosamente todo esto andado los idios la llaman guanahani. Ala segūda
puse nonbre la isla de santa maria deconcepcion ala tercera ferrandina ala quarta la isla bella
ala quita la Ysla Juana e asi a cada vna nonbre nuevo Quando yo llegue ala Juana seg
ui io la costa della al poniente y la falle tan grande q̄ pense que seria tierra firme la prouicia de
catayo y como no falle asi villas y luguares enla costa dela mar saluo pequeñas poblaciones
con lagente delas q̄ules nopodia haver fabla por que luego fuyan todos: andaua yo a de
lante por el dicho camino pēsado deno errar grādes Ciudades o villas y al cabo de muchas
leguas visto q̄ no havia inouaciō i que la costa me levava alsetētrion de adōde mi voluntad
era cōtraria porq̄ el yvierno era ya ēcarnado yo tenia proposito de hazer del al austro y tan biē
el viēto medio adelāte determine deno aguardar otro tiēpo y bolui atras fasta vn señalado puer
to de adōde ēbie dos hōbres por la tierra para saber si havia Rey o grādes Ciudades ādovi
erō tres iornadas y hallarō ifinitas poblaciōes pequeñas i gēte si numero mas no cosa de reg
imiēto por lo qual se bolvierō yo entēdia harto de otros idios q̄ ia tenia tomados como conti
nuamēte esta tierra era Ysla e asi segui la costa della al oriēte ciento i siete leguas fasta dōde fa
zia fin: del qual cabo vi otra Ysla al oriēte distīcta de esta diez o ocho leguas ala qual luego
puse nombre la spañola y fui alli y segui la parte del setentrion asi como dela iuana al oriente.
clxxviii grādes leguas por linia recta del oriēte asi como dela iuana la qual y todas las otras
sō fortissimas en demasiado grado y esta en estremo en ella ay muchos puertos enla costa dela
mar si cōparaciō de otros q̄ yo sepa en cristianos y fartos rrios y buenos y grandes q̄ es mara
villa las tierras della sō altas y ē ella muy muchas sierras y mōtañas altissimas si cōparaciō
de la isla de cētre frey todas fermosissimas de mil fechuras y todas ādabiles y llenas de arbols
de mil maneras i altas i parecen q̄ llegā al cielo i tēgo por dicho q̄ iamas pierdē la foia segun lo
puede cōphēder q̄ los vi tā verdes i tā hermosos como sō por mayo en spaña i dellos stavā flor
ridos dellos cō fruto i dellos en otro termino segū es su calidad i cātava el rui señor i otros pa
xaricos demil maneras en el mes de noviēbre por alli dōde io āndava ay palmas de seis o de
ocho maneras q̄ es admiracion verlas por la diformidad fermosa dellas mas asicomo los o
otros arboles y frutos eiervas en ella ay pinares amaravilla e ay canpiñas grādissimas e ay mi
el i de muchas maneras de aves y frutas muy diversas enlas tierras ay muchas minas deme
tales e ay gēte istimabile numero La spañola es maravilla la sierras y las mōtañas y las vegas
y las campiñas y las tierras tan fermosas y gruesas para plantar y sebrar pacuar ganados de to
das suertes para hedificios de villas e lugares los puertos dela mar aqui no havria chreencia sin
vista y delos rios muchos y grandes y buenas aguas los mas delos quales traē oro ē los arbo
les y frutos e yervas ay grandes differencias de aquellas dela iuana en esta ay muchas specie
rias y grandes minas de oro y de otros metales. La gente desta ysla y de todas las otras q̄ he
fallado y havido: ni aya havido noticia andan todos desnudos hōbres y mugeres asi como
sus madres los parē haun que algunas mugeres se cobrian vn solo lugar cō vna foia de yerv
a: o vna cosa de algodō q̄ pa ello fazen ellos no tienen fierro ni azero ni armas ni son par
a ello no por que no sea gente bien dispuesta y de fermosa estatura saluo que sō muy te[illegible]oroso
amaravilla no tienē otras armas saluo las [illegible] delas cañas quando estan cōla simiente
a la qual ponen al cabo vn palillo agudo e no [illegible] vsar de aqllas que [illegible] vezes [illegible]
[illegible] embiar a tierra dos o tres hombres alguna villa pa haver fabl[illegible] y sali[illegible]

Figure 1 Columbus Letter to Santángel (NY Public Library)

to move information, swiftly and securely, regarding products, prices, and opportunities, from where things happened to where decisions were made. Meanwhile, church and state officials sought the fastest and most efficient means to inform and be informed regarding important matters of policy and power. Private individuals were drawn into a new environment in which news was to have a hitherto unimagined place in lives and livelihoods. Persons of all sorts, for good or for ill, participated in the regular circulation of news, by writing, sending, and even inventing what was to become the talk of the day and the basis for behavior in every realm. Merchants, princes, diplomats, priests, scribes, even spies, were among the professional categories of some of the most productive individuals in this regard, some of whom we will encounter in this Element.

Not only the structures of the news system, but also the content, will be our subject here. The relevant literature has often tended to dwell on the writers, bearers and routes of news, with less attention to what readers actually might have read. Numerous projects providing easier access to archival material, including actual transcriptions of relevant documents, along with more easily accessible resources for studying early printed texts, often deploying advanced technology, have facilitated a more comprehensive approach (Raymond 2025: chaps 2, 7). A wide-ranging comparative perspective will also be attempted, combining the insights of numerous studies focused on the major European areas and languages, to discover what the news was, as well as how it was transmitted and received.

Studies on the history of news are abundant and growing in number, including Elements in this series, testifying to how far the topic in general has come, with respect to the past decades of relative oblivion or relegation to the realm of curiosities or local studies. Just in the past fifteen years, new initiatives have emerged, promising to apply new research methods to vast amounts of hitherto nearly inaccessible material. Based at the University of Vienna, the Fuggerzeitung project under the leadership of Katrin Keller, with help from Paola Molino and Nikolaus Schobesberger, aimed to digitize the entire collection at the Austrian National Library of handwritten newsletters directed to the Fugger merchant family in the sixteenth century and mark them up according to map locations, dates, and proper names.[2] Along somewhat similar lines, the EURONEWS Project, including the present author along with Sara Mansutti, Davide Boerio, Carlotta Paltrinieri, Wouter Kreuze, and others, aimed to transcribe and analyze the entire newsletter portion of the Medici grand ducal collection at the State Archive in Florence.[3]

Why the shift in perspective? What were once regarded as fatal flaws in the media of the past (and the present) and therefore reasons for dismissal from serious research are now regarded as vital points of interest. Recent work has carefully probed the signs of unscrupulousness, the evidence of haste, and drawn conclusions from these in regard to the nature of the business and the

---

[2] https://fuggerzeitungen.univie.ac.at/.   [3] https://euronewsproject.org/.

experience of those who participated in it, viewing these as key episodes in the history of the life of the times. Political, economic, and military values were at stake, and the survival of dynasties, states, and populations depended on what could be known or believed. Developing structures sustaining news – highways, mail routes, printing, and paper making enterprises – were some of the same as those sustaining states and populations more generally. Moreover, the news we find in our documents, at least as far as the texts are concerned, was inevitably the same as received by the people in the places where it reached. As a source for mentalities regarding the events of the day, it may well be unparalleled.

Readers at the time, as we shall see, were well aware of the defects and often complained about the inaccuracies, the inventions, the exaggerations, and even outright lies. Yet a widespread conviction persisted that however false or misleading a given story might be, a future story would set the record straight. No thorough study has been done to find out how often or how regularly this happened; and we will not undertake one here. But perhaps more important was the conviction that this defective product of the human mind was becoming a necessary accompaniment to daily life. Even the absence of news was an event worth recounting. Whether true or false, news was there to stay, and the world conjured up in story after story from place after place, marvelous in the Columbian case, or horrific in many other cases, and much in between, gave form and substance to the widening world view of early modern people.

This Element aims to provide a general overview of the topic, along with the significance and the current research terrain, regarding a phenomenon that developed and reached maturity between the fifteenth and the early seventeenth centuries. We will be tapping into a vast new bibliography, rich in discoveries about the persons, places and purposes of newsmaking. We will see how the first related activities took root in a few key centers at the beginning of our period, eventually multiplying and stretching from one end of Europe to another, before finally joining up with the other currents of momentous social, political and intellectual change that would make early modern society, for better or for worse, the gateway to modernity.

The discussion begins with the concept of news itself, the background of the term and its significance in the period. This is followed by the first of the three main vehicles of news in the Renaissance: namely letters. Forming the basis of medium- to long-distance communication for centuries, these reached a particular level of sophistication in the Middle Ages. Next comes a major offshoot: handwritten newsletters, which held sway for over a hundred years and formed the basis for one of the great inventions of the time, occurring at the end of our period: namely, printed newspapers. Of course, long before this, printed news in general, covered here in the last section, played a key role in informing about, triggering, and fomenting events and movements that occurred from time to time.

Considering recent transformations in perceptions of the world due to major developments in media technology (Habermas 2023), understanding the convoluted path from a distant media past to a truly overwhelming media present appears more relevant than ever.

1 What's News?

On the last day of Boccaccio's Decameron, the character "Panfilo" tells a story that seems to epitomize the state of international news flows at the dawn of the Renaissance. The Sultan of Babylon has heard about the Third Crusade and travels incognito around Italy and elsewhere to reconnoitre. The personally collected information about preparations being made for restoring Jerusalem to the Christian forces will be put to good use. "Being now fully informed," we are told, he went home and "addressed himself to his defence" (Boccaccio, ed. Marti and Valla 1981). At the time when Boccaccio wrote, the overwhelming news of the day was not about the crusades, but about the devastations wrought by the Black Death on populations throughout Europe, from which the "novelle" are framed as a welcome detour into the world of make-believe. In the following centuries the flow of news, real or imaginary, would assume an increasingly important role in peoples' lives.

Such a preoccupation with everyday affairs, while obviously necessary, was not always seen as worth celebrating, or even as ethically sound. Geoffrey Chaucer, author of the Canterbury Tales and an avid reader of Boccaccio, offers a somewhat darker view of information. In the Man of Law's tale (fragment II) certain merchants have gained the confidence of the Sultan of Syria by their activities as bearers of news from far and wide. Hoping for generous treatment by the Sultan, they seek out "tidyinges of sondry regnes" in order to be able to convey "the wonders that they myghte seen or heere" (Chaucer, ed. Benson 2008). Unfortunately, a chief piece of news regarding the beauty of the daughter of the emperor of Rome leads to a disastrous wedding proposal by the Sultan; whereupon the Sultan's mother, opposed to any match involving a Christian bride, kills her son and sets the bride adrift at sea. Curiosity may thus have terrible consequences. Curiosity is even more explicitly decried in the Manciple's tale (fragment IX), where Phoebus' wife takes a low-born lover, the crow reveals their secret, and Phoebus in a rage kills his wife. The moral: hold your tongue, and do not be the author "of tidynges, whether they been false or trewe." The issue would preoccupy moralists for years to come.

On a more intellectual note, humans' actions, said Thomas Aquinas a century before Boccaccio, were defective, "as the sins of man testify" (1975: ch. 91, 1–5). Therefore, excessive interest in those actions was necessarily deleterious. This conclusion in the *Summa Contra Gentiles* proceeded from an elaborate exercise in scholastic reasoning. "Our acts of choice have the character of multiplicity," explained Aquinas, "since choices are made of different things, by different people, in different ways." But this also meant that such acts were woefully mutable, because of "the instability of the mind, which is not firmly fixed on the ultimate end," and also because of "the fluctuating character of the things which provide our circumstantial environment." Only the divine will is "uniform, because by willing one object it wills all else, and it is immutable and without defect," an inference for which he referred the reader to Book One of his *Summa Theologica*.

Before new instruments of communication exercised an incisive influence on mental patterns throughout Europe, resistance to the "libido sciendi," the excessive desire to know, was a common theme. Young minds were made acquainted with the limits on what could and could not be sought already at the first encounter with the biblical account of the forbidden fruit. In the confessional literature, the human impulse to curiosity was often decried, especially regarding "not necessary things." The thirteenth-century theologian - Guillaume d'Auvergne had already elaborated at some length on the problem in his treatise called "De tentationibus et resistentiis" (On Temptation and Resistance) stipulating that "curiosity is the primary assailant of our rational virtue, that is, the sublime and noble virtue of understanding" (1591: 283).

But preoccupation with human affairs was becoming impossible to resist. The once-unhurried rhythms of village life that characterized the experience of most of humanity in this part of the world, were being swept up in the pace of change wrought by emerging urban commercial and power elites and the accompanying structures as never before. The associated requirements sparked people's need for, and apprehension of, the world around. Events were demanding attention. To those who may have heard about them, the travels of Marco Polo provided suggestions however vague about widening the boundaries of human consciousness and opportunities abroad, eventually to be realized in voyages of exploration eastward and westward, whereas the Black Death in 1348 began the (micro-) biological unification of the known world (Varlik 2015, Burgio 2024). The once-fixed boundaries of urban life were giving way to the uncertainties of more distant horizons. Long before modern "acceleration theory" (Rosa 2013), we might almost say that immobile history, to borrow a term from Emmanuel Le Roy Ladurie (1974), was giving way to mobile history.

The literary world took some time to adapt. Matteo Villani, an older contemporary of Boccaccio, began his chronicle of Florence with "how the world came to be inhabited after the confusion of the Tower of Babel" (1991: 2). But mixing the biblical with the mundane in telling about events, he attempted to demonstrate how the things above gave importance to those below. Only in the ninth book of his account, he began dealing with the early fourteenth-century conspiracy of Bajamonte Tiepolo in Venice, the appointment of Charles d'Anjou as Lord of Florence, eventually, amid the continuing struggles between Guelfs and Ghibellines, followed by Walter of Brienne, and so forth, allowing the larger themes to be framed, and often overwhelmed, by the minutiae of Florentine life.

Finally with Leonardo Bruni, writing in the early fifteenth century, humans and their accomplishments take center stage and undergo scrutiny as intense as in any of the ancient classics by Livy or Tacitus (Cochrane 1981: 5). Well aware of his novelty and the changing times, he asserts in the introduction to his History of Florence that "men of earlier ages" since antiquity, "whatever the extent of their learning and eloquence," instead of recording "the events of their own day," had allowed these to "pass by in silence" (2001: 5). Thus (he insists) the "memory of remarkable men and heroic actions has been almost wholly lost" in spite of, or due to, the chroniclers' misguided efforts. He therefore begins his history with "what I think is the most correct tradition concerning the city's founding and its origins" which "will involve rejecting some commonly held but mythical beliefs," considering that this "will shed light on what is to follow, when describing "the times that mainly concern me," namely, his own.

Especially in Bruni's accounts of causation, news plays a major role, mentioned no less than thirty times just in the last four books of his *History*, with terminology such as "nuntiabatur" (it was reported), "fama delatus est" (the word spread), and the like. For instance, in 1379 news arrives that a lieutenant of Charles of Anjou-Durazzo was approaching Tuscany with a band of exiles, so the city hires John Hawkwood as a military leader (2007: 19). In 1381 when Charles takes over the Kingdom of Naples, placing Queen Johanna in prison, the news causes such concern in Florence that the city immediately seeks to establish official relations with the new ruler, and news about the Florentine envoys' favorable audience in Naples reassures the Florentines. Later the same year news came from several sources saying that Louis, Duke of Anjou, was heading to Italy with an army; whereupon the Florentines set up defensive alliances with surrounding cities (2007: 51). In 1396, news arrives that an enormous host of knights from Milan was setting out for Tuscany to protect the Pisans, enemies of Florence; and hearing this, the Florentines send envoys to the Pisans and the Lucchesi urging them to reach an accord (2007: 209). Moving ahead a few years, in 1402, news about preparations for alliances among Italian states made by Giangaleazzo Visconti, Duke of Milan, shortly before his death, inspires hopes for a successful beginning to a new era of peace (2007: 299).

Bruni's attention to the dynamics of information among emerging and established states merely replicated what was occurring all around him, as the significance of events beyond local boundaries continued to challenge previous habits of looking only to neighborhood, city, and region. As long as perspectives were mostly bounded by local cityscapes and surrounding walls and fields (Harvey 1990), news did not have far to come or go, and could easily be exchanged by voice, especially at the regular times of greater confluence due to religious or civic observances. Town criers shouted out what was most important to hear, usually sent by the local authorities, with accompanying fanfare if the news was particularly important, such as an official decree. Specific local places became known as prime locations where news-related conversations were most likely to be found, usually around markets or public buildings: the Rialto and piazza S. Marco in Venice, piazza Navona in Rome, Dam square in Amsterdam, Notre Dame cathedral square in Paris, plaza del Arrabal in Madrid, Cheapside in London, and surrounding areas and establishments in each of these locations, and similar settings in other urban areas (Fox 2002: ch.7, De Vivo 2007: ch.3, Baars 2021: 10). Such places did not lose their role as sites of diffusion even as the news being diffused began to comprehend wider realities.

Visualizing the places of news required special efforts. For most people, at the start of our period, city plans, where available, were largely ornamental, and wider geographies mostly unknown. Place and space had long been constituted by a series of vectors, we might say, leading out to where necessities came in, requests went out, and interests were served, some better defined than others (Dubbini 2002). Power and money, in various reciprocal relations, drove increased efforts, especially among elites, to gain a more accurate, and supposedly more useful world picture, in the actual sense as well as the figurative. The rediscovery of Greek antiquity, driven in part by the presence in Italy of Greek scholars such as Manuel Chrysoloras, motivated interests also in Greek geographical knowledge as evidenced in the newly Latinized gazetteer of the Greco-Roman astronomer Ptolemy, which had already been enhanced in late medieval manuscripts of the work by scribal mapping exercises based on attempting to represent the Ptolemaic world along with later insights (Clemens 2008). The clearer picture would inform reports about events near and far.

Artists' conceptions of events featured realistic representations of current doers, deeds and donors in plain view where the public was invited. Leon Battista Alberti, in a treatise on painting drawing upon ancient principles, credited art with having power to "make the absent present" but also to represent "the dead to the living many centuries later, so that they are recognized by spectators with pleasure and deep admiration for the artist" (Alberti 1972: part 2, para. 25). Whatever the scene, humans were to be portrayed in lifelike poses, he suggested, often in the nude. The more intense the verisimilitude, the more likely to engage the emotions; hence the move toward ancient examples, with paintings from antiquity still mostly undiscovered in his time but sculptures and bas-reliefs intensively unearthed and displayed. Secular commissions abounded in every area of subject matter.

Of course, artists needed no reminding about the value of informative scenes, an important source of income as long as families, cities and countries had resources to commission them (Paret 1997). For depicting the various military enterprises then raging throughout Europe, some, such as the "Victory of the Sienese over the Florentines at Poggio Imperiale" (1480), painted by Francesco d'Andrea and Giovanni Ghini di Cristofano, appeared on walls of public buildings, in this case, the Palazzo Pubblico in Siena, so soon after the event as to constitute almost a form of visual news in themselves (Brandi et al. 1983). We see there depicted a key moment in the War of Siena when a coalition of papal, Aragonese and Sienese forces gained the advantage over the Florentines, done in monochrome but with lively detail and key figures labeled, such as the Duke of Calabria and the Duke of Urbino.

Public ceremonial was a key part of rule, as in all traditional societies (Geertz 1993), reminding subjects that the ruling elite was alive and well and able to motivate an entire city or country by a simple gesture, often in the company of local ecclesiastics. Capturing such moments was already a long artistic tradition. Weddings, birthdays, feast days, military victories, visits by key figures of church and state, called forth columns of appropriately clad individuals accompanied by music, military salutes, and an outpouring of public appreciation. Depictions mixed the sacred and the secular, as in Benozzo Gozzoli's Journey of the Magi (Acidini Luchinat 1993), ostensibly a biblical scene but actually referring to the arrival in town of Pope Pius II in 1458 and painted shortly afterward, to adorn a private chapel in the palace later known as Medici-Riccardi. There we find lifelike depictions of various figures from in and around the Medici court: Cosimo (Pater Patriae), Lorenzo the Magnificent, Piero (the Gouty), along with allies and their relations, such as Sigismondo Malatesta, Galeazzo Maria Sforza, and even scholars such as Marsilio Ficino and artists including Benozzo himself.

Accompanying the quickening pace of events and the need to distinguish the news from the old, was the emergence of mechanical timekeeping. Noted by David Landes (2000[2]) and Gerhard Dohrn-van Rossum (1996), the invention of escapements and oscillatory devices by anonymous medieval artisans probably in the thirteenth century but improved from then onward, placed the problems in a new context. Daily life, once structured around the change of seasons and the tolling of the canonical hours, would never be the same again. No more an ineffable reality, impossible to define and difficult to quantify, time seemed from henceforth to be a quantity not beyond the grasp of humans. Long before Heidegger pointed to the philosophical naiveté of the concept (Ricoeur 1984: vol. 3, chap. 3), a sequence of "nows" was beginning to shape the daily framework of pre-modern experience. By the fifteenth century, the question "when" could be answered with hitherto unimagined precision.

Access to news was by no means uniform within societies. What you knew about affairs within the corridors of power depended upon who you were. Indeed, statements regarding distribution and impact, usually by critics, lawyers or consultants to the various emerging state governments, took account of the deep social stratifications and differences in education that marked this age (Houston 2002: ch. 7). A lawyer or a doctor was likely to be better informed than a butcher or a baker. What you knew also depended on where you were; and not all cities were alike. Paris was better served by information than was Strasbourg. And the strands of urban Europe reached thinly from center to center across vast stretches of landscape, where the political environment seemed far less crucial than the natural environment to the daily practices of existence. And even though the passage of troops from one battle to the next, just as the movement of prices between boom and bust, could intrude profoundly into an otherwise self-contained and autarchic village culture, nevertheless, political knowledge and intelligence extended unevenly and with great difficulty beyond the great demographic concentrations.

Then and now, profound doubts persisted about connecting words to experience, and the best ways to do so. Ancient philosophers had covered such ground in influential ways, well known to early modern university students. Aristotle (Aristotle 1984), whose work on poetics was available in a Latin edition by Lorenzo Valla since 1498, notoriously preferred poetry to history. Writing exactly what happened, in other words, was not the highest form of literary expression. History and poetry obviously both involved putting deeds into words, responding to a universal human tendency to tell what happened; but greater pleasure could be derived from contemplating the actions of the world with a view to learning and inferring much more. Of the two, he says, only poetry offered the possibility of addressing universal truths, including those regarding things done or that might have been done.

Nonetheless, with the increasing importance and impact of news, a fictive approach could serve moral and philosophical purposes. Thomas More in his

Utopia ([1516] 1967) imagines having engaged in a discussion, during a diplomatic mission to Antwerp, between himself, a local friend, and a traveler recently returned from a long trip to faraway lands not yet known in Europe. In Book 1 of the work, topics ranged across various issues and problems of public order, viewed in a comparative perspective, with emphasis on merciful treatment of the unfortunate and encouragements to economic and social well-being. In Book 2, the traveler delivers his wide ranging description of what was seen and experienced in the marvelous land of Utopia, laying emphasis upon the wisdom of its popular government, the diligence of the inhabitants, the piety of its church. With tongue in cheek, the writer's friend in a fictive dedicatory letter exclaims that Amerigo Vespucci, in the land eventually to be called America, saw nothing worthy of comparison. Only a few years later Europeans would be treated to the first descriptions of the conquest of Mexico by Hernán Cortés. The contrast would be instructive.

At all social levels, in all places, the activity of telling about events encountered similar complications. No one yet suggested relegating the matter to the realm of unanswered metaphysical questions (more recently, Schulz 1976). But Torquato Tasso, before completing the epic poem *Jerusalem Delivered*, put emphasis on the fundamental fragility of news knowledge. In his 1582 treatise entitled *Il Messaggero* [the messenger] he claimed to instruct prospective diplomats or courtiers in the ways of the political world. He imagines a dialogue between himself and "the Spirit," a being apparently well acquainted with Plato's cave, viewed in a Christian context. Concerning worldly matters in general, says the Spirit, "down here [on earth] you see nothing true, nothing sincere and pure, nothing in the end solid or stable; but these things, which offer themselves to your senses, are ghosts (so to call them) of the real and images of those, which are truly essences, which you cannot see down here, because your intellectual eyes are clouded by the veil of humanity; but opening them in the other life, which alone is life, they will manifest themselves to you in such a way that you will laugh at your past deceptions" (Tasso 1582: 3 r). And supposing the truth could be grasped, what if might cause damage to oneself or others? Honest dissimulation was the rule.

None of the doubts or caveats could slow the pace of events or tame the efforts to keep up with them. What would be the point? Things happened; people wanted to know. Then, as now, there was no denying that narrating events is a universal human necessity and skill, applied to fiction and nonfiction alike. Where writers were to go with these distinctions, we shall soon see.

2 News in the Mail

Gherardo Bueri, merchant in Lubeck, Germany in 1446, well knew the advantages of good information. Writing to Giovanni de' Medici in Florence in August of that year, he reminds his correspondent about the details of an order of furs to be sent back to Italy, including sleeves made from Swedish marten pelts. "I ordered one of my associates at the fair in ... Geneva, to send you up to 60 so you are well served" (Melis 1972: 204). Meanwhile there is an opportunity to get sable and ermine from Russia, which have suddenly become more valuable than ever because of scarcities caused by the civil war. "The main land of Russia called Moscovy, is burning," he informs; "and where so many valleys are burned the ermines and sables are worth a fortune." When opportunity knocks, the merchant listens, and letters were the indispensable conduit for information of every sort.

As the Middle Ages waned and papermaking boomed, letters drove interests like never before, cementing relationships, demonstrating sincerity, confirming testimonies, even trying to mislead or just amuse (Martin 1988: ch. 7). The advantages over persistent orality for public and private uses were impossible to ignore, and the potential for covering distances was seemingly unlimited. Featuring date and place of writing, along with the name (or other indication) of the sender, they appeared to permit verification and confirmation of the information they contained. Brief formalities apart (Your Most Illustrious Excellency; I humbly kiss your hand) and pious references (an occasional cross at the top of the page), they delivered compliments and commands, along with notions about ideas and events. Among individuals involved with matters abroad, they were the next best thing to being close at hand, and in a rapidly expanding world, they appeared to hold the key to mastery over change.

Writing some ten years after Bueri sent his letter, Benedetto Cotrugli, a merchant and humanist from Ragusa in Venetian Dalmatia, asserted in his treatise on commerce that "The pen is such a noble and excellent instrument that it is most necessary not only for merchants, but also for every art, both liberal and mechanical." Although his "L'arte de la mercatura" (The Merchant's Art) was not published in his lifetime, the 1478 manuscript circulated widely before finally coming to press in 1573. There, Chapter 13 explained "How to Keep Writings in Mercantile Order." His meaning was unequivocal. "If you see a merchant who finds the pen burdensome, or who is ill-suited to using it, you can be sure he is not really a merchant" (Cotrugli [1573] 2016). Then comes the novelty of the treatise: "Not only must he have skill in writing, but he must also know how to organize what is written ... Because the merchant must not do all his business by memory, unless he be like King Cyrus, who could call by name each of the innumerable soldiers in his army."

Writing, he went on, allows us "not only to preserve and retain in memory what is agreed and carried out, but also helps avoid many disagreements, doubts and complaints," while also allowing literate men to "live thousands of years by committing to memory the glorious name and the illustrious deeds, which cannot happen without this wondrous instrument of the pen" (Cotrugli [1573] 2016). The chapter concluded with a mythological reverie: "Oh how indebted is the human generation to Carmenta, mother of Evander, who, as the ancients write, was the first to discover the use of the pen!" Finally, in terms of the more practical aspect, "we see continually what convenience comes from writing, if for nothing else than to communicate from one place to another and to give notice of things from one country to another, of things great and small." Attention was everything.

No wonder that the exercise and consolidation of power now seemed to depend on lines of written text. A decade after Cotrugli wrote his treatise, in 1489, a beleaguered King Henry VII of England wrote to the Earl of Oxford, John de Vere, explaining the situation across the channel in Brittany, where a French takeover of the duchy could threaten the new Tudor dynasty. It was one year into the reign there of a new duchess, and the English troops had been advancing on the town of Guingamp. "After the garrison of Frenchmen ... had certain knowledge of the landing of our army, they pulled down the banners ... and made it suitable to defend against a siege. However, as soon as they understood that our said army was journeying towards them, they vacated Gyngham [Guingamp], where our said army arrived on the Thursday before Palm Sunday and was received with a procession, lodged and refreshed in the town for four days" (Gairdner 1904: VI,125). Fortunately, the information showed, English crown interests were making progress.

The king's letter was forwarded to John Paston by his brother William Paston, both of them Norfolk gentry and friends of the Earl of Oxford, no doubt as a reminder about the wider context of the recent dynastic struggles in which the family had in one way or another been involved. A vast collection of such authentic writings was conserved as the family grew in prominence over time. To be sure, the Pastons did not exchange information only of such pith and moment. A considerable portion of the voluminous correspondence, analyzed meticulously by numerous scholars in modern times, was devoted to family minutiae, especially the family businesses of landholding and marrying well, along with legal claims, celebrations, parties and the like, all of which may be news of a sort, more intimate concerns of counsel and guidance to the younger relatives.

Not only the men, but the Paston women also conveyed their avid interest in the political, military and social matters in their vicinity and abroad in letters that have survived. On January 7, 1462, amid the dynastic quarrels of the time, Margaret Paston writes to her husband John concerning events near the homestead: "People around here begin to grow rowdy, and it is said here that my Lord Clarence and the Duke of Suffolk are coming down with certain other judges to try such people who are rumored to be riotous in this district. And also it is said here that a new rescue has been submitted in response to that which was done at the last shire court" (Watt 2004: 67). She believes false news is to blame: "such talk comes from the dishonest villains who want to spread rumours around the district." In July 1465 she writes to her eldest son John II, who happens to be in Hellesdon, warning that "I am reliably informed that the Duke of Suffolk is building up a large force in both Norfolk and Suffolk to come down with him and drive us back, if they can." She entreats him "to use any means to make yourself as secure as you can in the place." And again, to the same, some ten years later, on May 23, 1475) she writes, "The King is so hard on us in this district, both poor and rich, that I do not know how we shall live unless the world reforms ... We can sell neither corn nor cattle for a good price" (Watt 2004: 111). Details follow: "Malt is only 10d per coomb here, wheat 28d per coomb, oats 10d per coomb. And there is little to be had here at the moment." On the other hand, she notes, "I am surprised that I have heard no news from you."

Collections of letters actually published by women at this time, paying tribute to the widely recognized revival of letters (in the larger sense) rarely included much about news, favoring instead thoughts more elevated and, considering the time required for printing, perhaps less stale (Zarri 1999). Traces remain, however, even in these sources, of the impact of news felt by the writers and presumably also the letter recipients. For instance, Veronica Franco, in her collection published in 1580, in the midst of wide-ranging European wars and revolts, writing to her sister claims that the things of the world were not ordered under a perpetual law similar to the invariable nature of the celestial movements, but rather, arranged so actions could be performed in many different ways and with different rules (1580: 25–27). Thus, depending on whether such matters were directed well or badly, by prudence or by little judgment, the results could be beneficent or catastrophic. However, Chiara Matraini writing in 1595 sounds a more positive note, insisting that "Those, then, will be very good and valiant warriors and worthy of true honor, who, following the best sciences, will strip themselves of ambition, hatred, rapine and vainglory of this world and of all their immoderate affections and desires, and will arm themselves with faith, justice, charity and all virtuous habits, and will overcome, with these most powerful weapons, their internal and external enemies" ([1595] 2018: 114).

A word of caution was in order: "although I believe that few of these are found," nevertheless such existed, and if they prevailed, "there would be peace, quiet and a most joyful union" among people.

In spite of the correspondence boom, writing and reading remained precious abilities in short supply and unevenly distributed geographically, by gender and across social groups. The two skills also did not necessarily coincide, nor, as Michel de Certeau points out, were they learned in the same way (de Certeau 1984: ch. 12). At the most elementary level, deciphering texts came before reading, and both could exist without writing. Women, it is thought, when they were literate at all, were more likely to receive instruction in reading, especially for religious purposes, than in writing, with the latter feature reserved for those in the family regarded as being more directly involved in extended actions beyond self and family (Goody 1977: 8–10, 15–17). Percentages are hard to come by, and the evidence from, for instance, signatures on documents, or books in a probate inventory, may not tell much about literacy at all. Nonetheless, using a variety of approaches, one gender-unspecific estimate puts literacy in the larger cities of mid sixteenth-century Italy at around 20 percent and rising, with other areas, including parts of Elizabethan England, rapidly catching up (Cressy 1980, Buringh and Van Zanden 2009). Among all other agents of change in literacy over our period the Protestant Reformation was surely the most effective, along with the cultural, social, religious and military consequences of this (Houston 2002: chap. 2).

What qualified as letter writing, and among whom? Amid the myriad stylistic variations, basic letter format was governed and disciplined largely by the education of those who wrote, sometimes based on time-tested usage over recent centuries, sometimes grounded in the classic texts of Cicero and Quintillian, reduced to precepts in schools (Mack 2011: chap. 11). In the time after the invention of the neolatin letter within Poggio Bracciolini's circle in the early fifteenth century, the possible reach of even the correspondence of a private individual could be quite considerable. Indeed, the emerging "republic of letters," to use a term reproposed by Desiderius Erasmus in 1494, was a particularly resonant echo chamber for news among the better educated elite, with accounts of all sorts circulating in artful Latin phrases (Burke 1999). Erasmus himself was among the principal protagonists in his day, along with his correspondent, the French scholar Guillaume Budé.

The Erasmus correspondence network was not simply a means for moving letters from place to place, but for joining intellectuals from very distant locations into a single system. Rendered convincingly in visual terms by Christoph Kudella (2016), the system in fact reached over the more and more clearly defined state boundaries, crossed increasingly fraught confessional lines, followed scholars in their peregrinations, so that the locations of the nodes might change, with the edges and directions back and forth between the central figures and the rest remaining firm. At last count the letters sent and received from 1484 to 1536 amounted to nearly three thousand, including some 2,000 directed to Erasmus by some 700 correspondents from 202 locations all over Europe: 109 from Basel, 65 from Paris, 58 from Louvain, 55 from London, and so forth. The particularly voluminous Basel contingent can be explained by many friends there due to long sojourns in the city of his main publisher, Johann Froben. Other nodes included Pierre Gilles, Thomas Linacre, Andrea Alciati, King Francis I, and, of course, Guillaume Budé.

Serving as a background to the lofty subjects of intellectual and theological interest and the trivia of personal concerns in the Erasmus correspondence, we find the momentous and sometimes monotonous succession of events driven by authorities in church and state and their constituencies. Letters are scattered with requests for "what news there is from England" [ecquid ab Anglis noui] and the like. In return Erasmus offers what he has: "If you are looking for news from me," he reports from Brussels some time in July 1498, "I can add that the supreme pontiff has sent to our archduke the splendid gift of a golden rose, the workmanship of which is far more remarkable even than the material" (1906: 320). And again, "the pope with the help of the French army was preparing to besiege Bologna," he reports from Florence in November 1506, "But now . . . it is reliably reported that Bentivoglio has been caught by the French as he fled with three of his sons" (Erasmus 1906: 431). As a consequence he was making new travel plans: "I hope that the situation will settle down and allow me to return to Bologna, where the pope and his cardinals are to winter." In the case of a highly mobile scholar such as Erasmus, news and the associated events could impinge dramatically on life and work.

For any letter writing, in Latin or in the increasingly widespread vernacular tongues, certain events, especially involving violence in wartime, called for special efforts to get the message across. Things were happening which defied even the most precise verbal accounts. For achieving accuracy, personal observation could be misleading. This Erasmus himself noted in the fifth dialogue of his *Colloquies*, first issued in the printed edition of 1522. For rendering the reality of a typical battle where the tumultuous barrage included "blasts of trumpets, thunder of horns, neighing of horses and clamor of men" any observer was severely challenged (Erasmus 1997: 53). Distractions abounded at the sites of a struggle – not least because of the necessity for each observer to seek sudden shelter from dangers emerging unexpectedly. When Hanno, one of the interlocutors in the dialogue, asks about how it was, the other, a certain Thrasymachus, supposedly just returned from the Italian wars, replies that "I couldn't see what was going on, as I scarcely knew where I was myself."

The particular hazards of war reporting had not changed by 1527, as Sigismondo da la Torre discovered in the midst of the action taking place on November 6 during the sack of Rome. "The men-at-arms were supposed to leave," he says in a letter to the Marquis of Mantua, "but they mutinied, and although many efforts were made to satisfy them, there was still no order; today they have to be summoned and begged to take four ducats apiece as a subsidy; but it is believed that they will not do so" (Sanuto [Sanudo] 1879–1904, vol. 48, col. 193-4). Descriptions alternate with partial explanations in rapid fire. "The reason why they mutinied was their resentment for having been given permission to go and lodge in Nepi, and then the order was revoked and the Spanish infantry was sent to lodge there instead; so from then on, they began to show what perhaps they previously had in mind, having always complained about mistreatment." With no agreement forthcoming things could only get worse, but help might be on the way. "They say they want to enter the kingdom [of Naples] at once. We hope for the best concerning the things of His Holiness, nor do we expect anything other than the return of the secretary Serrone who must settle the accounts within three days." Next comes a series of conjectures echoing Hanno's doubts in the *Collioquies*. "It has been said here that the camp of the league has retreated to Foligno, and the French who had already crossed the Po have turned back: some say new reserves of Germans are coming, some say to take Milan, having foreseen the designs of the His Holiness, and others say, to sue for peace, which has practically been concluded between the Emperor and the Most Christian King." Obviously in this as in other cases, distance equals uncertainty. "But I don't write these things except to show how things are going here, because I know you already know better where you are" – presumably, further up the peninsula. The difficulties by no means discouraged the attempts to get the message across.

The letter concerning the Sack of Rome has survived by way of a transcription within the remarkable 58-volume diary from those times, written by Marino Sanudo, Venetian patrician and member of the Great Council, whose accounts consisted largely of communications from wherever Venetian officialdom managed to make contact, plus miscellaneous information from a variety of sources. A considerable portion of the material was read aloud during Council meetings and apparently transcribed in loco by the diarist. Thus, a typical diary entry from volume 53 for the first of March 1530, refers to letters having arrived from Bologna, Ferrara, Cividale di Friuli, and Florence (borne in person by the messenger), with topics ranging from the health of the Duke of Milan, the relations between the Duke of Ferrara and the Pope, the Turkish incursion into Cozevia and

Ribaniza, and the siege of Florence by the Imperial army (Sanuto [Sanudo] 1879–1904, vol. 53, cols. 5–7). Entries over the following two days featured a letter from Curzola, four letters from Bologna, and one each from Constantinople, Monopoli, Ferrara, and over the month of March 110 in all, some merely mentioned, some given in full from the oral delivery or from the letters themselves. For the entire period between 1496 and 1533, entries refer to some 10,000 items received, including over a thousand from Rome, 871 from Milan, 812 from Lyon, 682 from Naples, 672 from London, and between 30 and 60 each from Candia, Damascus, Cairo and so on, testifying to a Venetian government intensely interested in world affairs. No one could ignore the importance of staying up to date.

More and more, the business of rule involved the sending and receipt of such correspondence (Petitjean 2013: Introduction). In 1550s Florence, Cosimo I de'Medici, Duke of Florence, soon to become grand duke of Tuscany, was receiving over 5600 letters for a single four-year period, from 364 identifiable locations, including, just to mention the places outside Italy: Altdorf, Antwerp, Amiens, Angers, Augsburg, Avignon, and down through the alphabet to Hadrianopolis, Halle, and eventually Zara (Archivio di Stato di Firenze 1990). Later in the century Philip II received the sobriquet "King of Paper," for his attention to the mail; and by 1590 quite apart from the letters having been read, he reportedly had written enough to constitute more than four mule loads of used paper. But the real weight was on himself, as he occasionally complained. "I have 100,000 papers in front of me," began a note to a secretary (Parker 2014: 75). On another occasion he assured his personnel that "So far I have been unable to finish with these devils, my papers, but I am taking some with me to read in the countryside, which is where I am headed right now" (tr. in Parker 2014: 114).

Court and administrative officials specifically assigned to manage the exchange of information emerged in every state, distinguished at least in part by their expertise rather than, as before, almost exclusively by blood ties or servitude to a dynasty or prominent family. For providing a constant flow of information about events going on in and around an assigned destination, instructions by rulers to their envoys and representatives were everywhere alike. Those given by Cosimo de' Medici's staff to Fabritio Ferrari, sent by Cosimo from Florence to the court of Ferrando Gonzaga, governor of Milan, in 1552, were clear and precise: "Your main care and responsibility must be to inform us continuously about the war in Piedmont, the necessities of the state of Milan, and about everything else in the area that you consider to be worthy of our notice" (Contini and Volpini, eds. 2007: 181). Also included in the list of things worthy of attention were "any fresh information from the court of the emperor [Charles V], of the practices and handling that will be understood of the

Swiss, and of all the others." He added, "Please note that it will seem expedient to tell us anything else worthy of our notice that we might not know, using your usual diligence and care."

Private secretaries to rulers became a specific profession, discussed in treatises by Torquato Tasso and others. Francesco Sansovino, son of the famous architect and a literary figure in his own right, published a treatise *"Del Segretario"* ["Concerning The Secretary"] outlining the epistolary techniques necessary for narrating an event. Innovating slightly on the classic "septem circumstantiae" (seven circumstances) explained in Cicero and Quintillian, he suggests that "such narratives must include the person who does, what was done, when was it done, where it was done, the way it was done, and the reason [why] it was done" (1584: 53v, Monti 2019, Kittler 2020). Of course, the particular rank and role of the recipient must be taken into consideration, as details are revealed concerning the thing which was to be communicated, whether public or private, regarding peace or war, at home or abroad, as well as the time in which such a thing occurred. He imagines a scenario in which a certain Giulio is supposed to tell a certain Tomaso about the war being carried out against the Turks. He might say: "When we were in public discussion we got letters from Hungary, whereby we understood that the Turks invading the entire countryside put everything to iron and fire. And the Senate hearing about this decided that everyone should give their opinion about whether to make peace or war with the Turks. And when everyone had given their opinion about the matter, the decision was taken, to make war against the Turks, and thus Sforza was made the Captain of that endeavor. And he has already provided arms and provisions, so in a few days we expect he will start moving." As always in such communications, demonstration of the correct attitude to the event is expected, such as, "please pray God to favor our plans, so our city will not only be saved, but will increase in greatness and power," thus indicating the sender's allegiance and cementing the relationship to the recipient.

Quite apart from the various secular interests so far discussed, some of the best-established global networks reputedly belonged to the religious orders, whose scriptoria drew upon a tradition dating back to the sixth-century practice endorsed by Cassiodorus. The emergence of the Jesuits in 1540 signified the elevation of ecclesiastical correspondence to a global scale as the basis for a massive conversion project (O'Malley 2004). The order's exercise in Asia, the Americas, and Europe counted over a thousand persons at the death of Ignatius of Loyola in 1556. Writing to their home colleges, they attempted to articulate not only the ways and means of conversion, but also the experiences of religious difference, along with customs and usages, often structuring their descriptions according to categories that recipients could be presumed to share.

The Jesuit Father Manuel da Nóbrega, for instance, writing from Bahía in Brazil to the Portuguese "College of Coímbra" in 1549, mentions the local view on the history of the world, in these terms: "They remember the Flood, but falsely, because they say that when the earth was flooded with water, a woman and her husband climbed up a pine tree, and when the waters receded and the earth was dry, came down and from them were born all the humans" (Samoes 1990: 346). Such was the task ahead, his readers might have thought, to correct similar errors by reference to the actual biblical account. Again, "They are very attached to sensual things; many times they have asked me, does God have a head and body, and [does he have] a woman, and how does he dress, and things of this kind." Information about the world signified acquaintance with realities never known before, inevitably conveyed with some interference from the culture of the writer.

For any clergy or laity interested in keeping track of events far away for any reason whatsoever, the task was never easy. Distance was "the first enemy," Fernand Braudel aptly said in an exhaustive work on the Mediterranean and the Mediterranean world in the age of Philip II (Braudel 1972: 355ff); and ways to overcome this were challenged by geography as well as infrastructure. Problems of transmission and reception gave rise to numerous *topoi* in letter-writing rhetoric, picked up by Braudel: "I am waiting for the regular Flanders mail to go past at any hour," wrote one correspondent (1972: 356); another pointed out that mail from France was slow because "many [letters] have remained at Burgos coming from the direction of Valladolid." Yet another called out "the knavery and negligence of the postmasters" as a cause of delays.

Ideally, a letter could take a day and a half to travel, say, from Venice to Rome by express courier. On the other hand, mail to Europe from Goa in Portuguese India went in and out only once per year, calling for appropriate adjustments in expectations and strategies. Annales school historian Pierre Sardella (1949) calculated the mean times of letters arriving at Venice from near and far, based on evidence in Sanudo's diary. Particular cases included Damascus, with arrival times varying from 28 to 102 days, depending on the weather or other impediments, with an average time of 80 days. Next in order of awkwardness came Cairo, with arrivals in 20 to 99 days, averaging 72, Alexandria, with arrivals in 17 to 89 days, averaging 65, and, from the opposite direction, Lisbon, arriving in 27 to 69 days, averaging 46, or London, between 9 and 52, averaging 27. Within Italy the longest waits could be twenty days from Naples, averaging, however, 9 days.

For devising more efficient routes and methods, much was at stake – not only from the standpoint of the basic public and private need to react in a crisis. The developing social and economic structures of a postmedieval world were at risk. Sardella (1949: 41–45) was able to show how prices and insurance costs in Venice fluctuated in relation to the major geopolitical upheavals, near and far – obviously conveyed in writing. Controlling for seasonal fluctuations and other possible circumstantial modulations, for instance, evidence shows that expectation of scarcities in grain exports due to the events of the Italian Wars and disruptions in Mediterranean trade affected by events in the Near East appeared to push prices up, while the resolution of disagreements seemed to have the opposite effect. In this last connection, the 1503 peace between Venice and the Turks is said to have pushed rising grain prices back down; incidentally coinciding also with the end of a cycle of contagious disease, seen as a favorable omen within a society wishing to placate the divine forces at work. The same year, news that the galleys had returned from Alexandria with less than the expected quantity of spices led to a rise in the price of pepper (Sardella 1949: 35). Even the "market" for ecclesiastical benefices (Sardella suggests) was now driven by information concerning the deaths or illnesses of current incumbents which might offer opportunities to a future candidate.

No wonder that by Sanudo's time the value of improved infrastructure for transmitting news of all kinds was coming to be appreciated as never before. All previous systems, so far as anyone knew, had been unable to keep abreast of all that was happening in the realms of warfare, popular unrest, visual arts, architecture, economic opportunities, ceremonial, and even mysterious portents across such a wide and expanding geographical spread. The ancient Roman world's informational pipeline, the cursus publicus, was long gone, and before the period studied by Sardella, news could take up to thirty days to reach Rome from Liège. For improving transit times, sufficient relays were necessary along the way for feeding and changing horses and riders. Local arrangements in Italy set the pace, first in Rome and Venice. A Venetian Company of Couriers organized themselves as a private group of mail carriers, paying a substantial sum of money for the right to manage some of the major routes in and out of the state, along with the right to collect the relevant fees. Meanwhile, the Venetian government developed regular courier services to Venetian Dalmatia and the Ottoman Empire (Caizzi 1992: 211–262).

Among the most successful and eventually the widest ranging delivery networks was the one established on behalf of the Habsburg Empire by the Tasso family, eventually known as Thurn und Taxis (Behringer 2003: 14–15). Originally from Bergamo and active at first in and around Lombardy, they were on hand in Northern Europe just as the imperial territories began to coalesce into a vast system spanning the continent from Austria to Iberia under Maximilian I and Charles V. Each expansion brought new communications challenges, and in return for regular payments, privileges and titles, the Tasso family pledged to build routes throughout these territories, with links to local carriers where necessary (Caplan 2016: chap. 1). Among the first regular transits in the new system ran from Innsbruck to Brussels, guaranteeing that the mail between the main imperial residences in Austria and the Low Countries, arrived in less than five days. By mid-century the route to Spain from Rome passed through Florence, Piacenza, Turin, Chambéry, and Narbonne (Arblaster 2006).

A major development with enormous consequences for the shape of news was the establishment of regular delivery times. E. J. B. Allen (1972: 37–39) records that for instance mail to England in the 1560s left Venice every Saturday for a certain period, later changed to Thursday. Mail arrived in Madrid from Constantinople generally every two weeks by a combined sea and land route. Depending on the circumstances the times could be shortened or lengthened; in the latter case, between 1583 and 1591 on the Lyon-Italy line, from bimonthly to monthly. More reliable mails increased the incentive to communicate; and predictable departure times not only helped correspondents pace their correspondence activity accordingly, but went far in shaping administrative, business, and home activity according to a weekly or bimonthly schedule. A veritable "media revolution" was under way, in the words of Wolfgang Behringer (2006), which would gain added momentum with the general diffusion of the newly invented anonymous handwritten newsletters.

By the end of our period the system crossed the length and breadth of Europe (see Figure 2), meeting the needs of a host of communities (for an overview, Joad Raymond 2025: 99–132). Ottavio Codogno dedicated the last hundred pages of his *Nuovo Itinerario delle Poste* (1608), to the "Departure of the Ordinary" mails, principally from Rome to elsewhere, but including a vast array of other routes. For instance, every Saturday night a rider went from the office of the Spanish ambassador and followed a route through Ronciglione, Monte Fiascone, Viterbo, Bolsena, Acquapendente, Radicofani, Siena, Florence, Bologna, Modena, and Mantua. In this last place, notes Codogno (1608: 329), "he leaves the bundles directed to Germany and Flanders," and continues with the rest "from Mantua to Cremona, Lodi, and Milan." After deliveries, the remaining bundles are placed "in a trunk and mounted on a carriage directed to Trent, Bolzano, Innsbruck and Augsburg," where the material is made available to the addressees, except for what is bound for Regensburg, Pilsen and Prague, now sent on its way.

Along these routes, Codogno showed, major hubs were joined by a series of intermediate stops or 'posts' (hence our expressions "the post" and even "going postal"). There riders could take refreshment and feed or change horses to be able to cover four to six such stops per day amounting to a total of 75–100 kilometers. For instance, between Lyon to Blois, he counted no fewer than

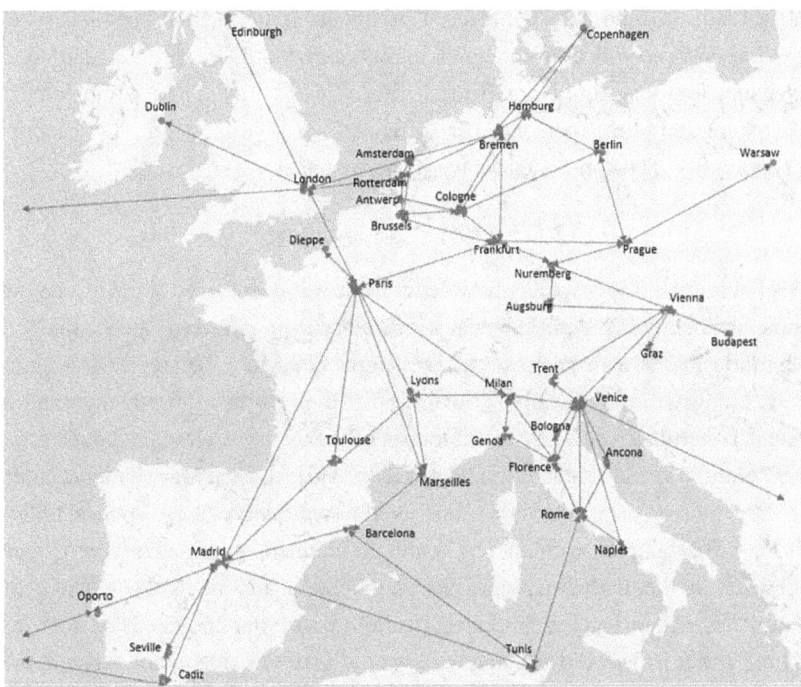

Figure 2 The European postal system in the early seventeenth century

twenty-three such stops including places cryptically referred to as "the Tower,'" or "the fountain on the way over the mountain of Tarara," and a location "at the crossing of the Lovera river," and so forth. The route from Rome to Spain involved 107 posts in all. Delivery services might, of course, be subject to delays from bad weather and military activity as well as highway robbery. But the same might occur in the case of the costly private couriers. Thus, by the public systems merchants sent and received mail as well as did authorities in Church and state and anyone else who needed to convey information for getting things done.

Lucien Febvre credits roads with having played a major role in the development of states and not vice versa (1966, Plebani 1999). But surely, the news that traveled along those roads played a particularly important role in forming the structures, practices, and mental horizons necessary for building fully articulated polities capable of resisting disaster and even perhaps profiting from the military revolution then under way (Parker 1996), which would change the face of Europe. Considering the urgencies experienced and the interests involved, there is no wonder that regular news reporting developed pari passu with regular mail. Entrepreneurs, as we might call them, recognized the opportunities at an early stage. In time there emerged a particular genre, a news medium so to speak, easily recognizable and quick to produce, suited for wide distribution in exchange for money or favors. Hitherto regarded as a duty or an accompaniment to other activities, personal or official, news was about to become a commodity. The consequences were enormous, as we shall see.

3 Dawn of the Newsletter

The February 8, 1556, weekly newsletter from Venice received at the Florentine court of Cosimo I (Figure 3) began with a story from Antwerp dated January 5 regarding things then going on in England. "The Most Reverend Monsignor Pole, along with the bishops, is waiting for the reform of that Kingdom," it began, referring to one of the protagonists of the Roman Catholic rebound after the Reformation headed in England by Henry VIII.[4] Queen Mary had just taken up the crown on the death of the short-lived Edward VI, with her spouse, Philip II, king of Spain, as co-ruler. The writing continued, stating that "The Queen obtained in the Parliament the power to create and nominate a Duke of Lancaster, which Duchy continued in the crown after the death of John of Gaunt, and it is believed that she will want to give this title to her husband the King." Catholic hopes were advancing, and there was much speculation about where things might go from here.

The information gave a tiny glimpse into the political and diplomatic situation in a crucial moment, seemingly described by someone relatively close to the events in question or who had contact with someone at the scene. The salient points about the currently tense political climate in England and Europe are in full view, rife with possibilities but also with dangers, as Catholics and Protestants continued locked in a struggle for supremacy that affected lives, property, and culture, with no end in sight in spite of the occasional treaties and truces. Dynasties are apparently forming new alliances with unknown consequences, but commentary is reduced to a minimum due to space limitations, leaving readers to form judgments on their own. Nonetheless there was enough here for the document to deserve all the care lavished upon it and the other newsletters received across two centuries by the Medici court and now preserved in some 200 volumes at the state archive in Florence (Barker 2016). To understand the importance for the history of Renaissance news we must go beyond this document to the phenomenon as a whole.

Forged in the previous half-century from a hybrid of diplomatic and commercial correspondence, newsletters soon became a genre on their own (Infelise 2002: ch. 1–4). In the document at hand, the report on Queen Mary was

---

[4] Archivio di Stato, Florence [=ASF], Mediceo del Principato [=MdP], vol. 3079, fol. 13r.

Figure 3 February 8, 1556, newsletter (Florence: Archivio di Stato)

followed by others on other topics, organized by place of origin and date of story. After Antwerp came Rome, then Rimini, Milan, Ferrara, Brescia, Augsburg, Brussels, Constantinople, "France," and, finally, dated February 8, a report from Venice. This last place and date no doubt referred to the writer's location at the moment, an alternative to another common practice of beginning a newsletter with the story closest to home. The two folios would have been folded three times with an address on one side and a wax seal on the other, as was the custom in an age before envelopes, with variations, vaguely prefiguring twentieth-century airletters.

Newsletter contents ranged across the varieties of human experience, with accounts of major marriages, births, illnesses, and deaths, as well as military engagements and popular revolts, miraculous signs and portents, geographical discoveries, new works of art, of architecture, of literature. The common element was novelty. News, as we have seen, had to be relatively fresh to be worthy of the name. A touch of irony occasionally lightened up the more serious fare, as in our newsletter from Venice, where among the last things read by Duke Cosimo's secretary there would have been an item stating that "The Cortinese nephew of" the previously mentioned "Most Reverend Pole who was practically the King of England, has come here," that is, to Venice, "and the reason for this is unknown." While picking through the mass of material for particularly pungent examples can be highly rewarding, new approaches also allow us to gain a more accurate overview of concepts shared over many years and across wide geographical areas.

From the researcher's standpoint, another common element in the newsletters, apart from those already mentioned, was rootedness in the Zeitgeist, that is, relevance to the particular concerns of a time distant to our own in spite of any occasional sense of familiarity, giving the modern reader an overall sense of being a stranger in a strange land. The same Venice section of the just-quoted newsletter concluded with a report that "the Duke of Florence is looking for all the alchemists who can come before him, and he makes them large offers and promises good salaries," although few are arriving, presumably because of the high demand for verified gold-making expertise in an age of ballooning state expenditure.

By the time of our example, the sheets had begun to circulate on a weekly or semi-weekly basis, making them the first such regular vehicles for news (Pettegree 2014: 1–17). The significance was enormous. No longer was news to be published mostly when it happened, haphazardly, sporadically, urged on only by the possible impact of the story or the interests in play, or as part of a monthly or biannual publication related to trade fairs or other occasions. Now there was to be a weekly format that demanded to be filled by writers whether there was big news or not, and that demanded to be read by anyone wishing to be informed, regardless of any particular expectations. No wonder the invention proved durable, and before the gradual disappearance of this genre in the eighteenth century many developments proceeded from there, as will be seen, in the realm of print.

The norms and practices of the newsletter business developed gradually over time, reaching maturity well into the sixteenth century (Barbarics-Hermanik 2012, Baars 2021: 16–17, Lamal 2023: chap. 1, Droste 2018: 103–145). There were no specific handbooks such as those available for other professions, but much can be inferred from the latter. Manuals for diplomats and secretaries, such as those by Ermolao Barbaro, Francesco Sansovino and Torquato Tasso, carried important relevant directions in the course of explaining the task of communication (Biow 2002). No doubt, those working at various levels of diplomatic activity had the means and interest to be involved in newsletter practice, even if this was not originally envisioned as a central part of an envoy's activities. However, providing a constant flow of information about events going on in and around the assigned destination by this time was everywhere required.

A common theme leading many diplomats down the path to newsletter activity was the necessity to give information to informers in order to receive more in return. Machiavelli therefore, in 1522, compiling the Florentine republic's instructions to Raffaello Girolami, the new ambassador to emperor Charles V, specified: "Your job is to write immediately and give notice of your arrival and of what you have explained to the emperor and of his response," he insisted, and you must then "write in detail about the affairs of the kingdom and the qualities of the prince, when, having been there for a few days, you will have specific information about them" (Machiavelli [1522] 2007). Meanwhile, he said, you must frequent the halls of state to any extent possible, in order to discover the nature of the emperor himself and the imperial entourage as well as any new enterprises currently under discussion. But in order to gain material there must be material to give, "because in the courts for various reasons there are always individuals doing this and that who try to understand what is going on around them," therefore "it is very appropriate to make friends with these in order to be able to find things out." Keep in mind, he adds, that "whoever wants others to tell him what they know, needs to tell others what he himself knows," so being informed of what was going on "in Bologna, Siena or Perugia ... and [knowing] what there is to say of the Pope, of Rome, of Lombardy, of the Kingdom [of Naples]" could be crucial "even if they are far from your affairs." Newsletter writers, whether diplomats or not, had to behave in a similar way regarding information.

In Rome, connected with the halls of church and state, and often appearing in the documents as authors of newsletters or, at the very least, as enablers of the practice, were the members of another profession with special rules and requirements: namely, the notaries. As "brokers for the public trust," in the interpretation of Laurie Nussdorfer (2009: ch. 2), they were supposed to dedicate responsible attention to the creation, formulation, certification and conservation of public written documents with legal significance, including contracts, wills and much else. Often the office of a successful member of the closed group of thirty Capitoline notaries included, for instance, a team of scribes capable of writing up numerous documents of many kinds, associated with the core activities of the office. Some of these scribes and occasionally minor notaries not connected with the top thirty are known to have rounded out their incomes by some activity as newsletter writers, or, at least, copiers of such. How many others in the bureaucracies of other states may have turned to such activity as an aspect of their special relation to truth is still uncertain (Burns 2005, Gallagher 2024).

Like most documents of its kind, our 1556 newsletter from Venice bears no signs of authorship. Featuring only a place and date as the heading, and lacking any of the usual epistolary formalities, newsletters were compiled and distributed by respectable officials in government and ecclesiastical bureaucracies as well as a motley assortment of lawyers, notaries, scribes, literary hacks, spies, unemployed intellectuals, and anyone inclined to produce one to four pages of news in exchange for money or favors or other goods. Although the newsletter business never emerged as an officially recognized trade except in terminology such as "reportista" (reporter), "menante" (bearer) or "novellante" (novel or news writer), the news product itself, under the name of "avviso," or even "gazzetta," as well as "geschriebene Zeitung," "nouvelles à la main," including all the printed varieties, nonetheless became a commodity, as Ben Jonson pointed out in *The Staple of News* – a commodity, we might add, just like any other in some ways, but also quite different (Arblaster et al. 2016, Infelise 2018).

Throughout the nearly two centuries in which newsletters flourished, anonymity remained the rule, with numerous exceptions (for exceptions, apart from those named herein, see De Vivo 2007: 88–89, Barbarics-Hermanik 2010 and 2012, Pettegree 2014: 330–331, Behringer 2017: 330–331). Various reasons could be suggested for the hiding of identity. For instance, we might point to the need to protect the writers in a regime of control over all types of writing. Another possibility could be the quest for a vague suggestion of indifference in respect to the various points of view that often entered into the reporting from one place or another, especially in the newsletters compiled from numerous accounts of various origins including letters, printed reports, and other newsletters. Busy writers and scribes, we might imagine, had little time to forge a particular editorial personality, and might studiously seek to avoid revealing a particular political slant. However, political opinions indeed emerge (Kreuze 2023), as we shall see, and a few identifiable figures, or nearly so, stand out as writers, largely due to the efforts of historians to recover this still little-known chapter of media history.

One such figure is Cosimo Bartoli, studied in the context of the IRC-funded EURONEWS Project and recently the object of a study by Sara Mansutti (2024). A prominent figure in intellectual circles around Italy from the early sixteenth century, Bartoli published among other things a treatise on measuring distances. Particularly remembered are his translations from Latin into vernacular Italian of works by the fifteenth-century author and architect Leon Battista Alberti, such as the *De Statua* and the *De architectura*. A staunch partisan of the Medici, he was chosen by Cosimo I to serve as Florentine resident in Venice, where he remained, with some interruptions, from 1562 until 1572, the year of his death in Florence. The newsletter from Venice, with its various stories from Antwerp and elsewhere, was included in an archival folder containing many documents written by him.

An unusually abundant supply of Bartoli's newsletter productivity has survived, catalogued as diplomatic missives or even as newsletters within the Mediceo del Principato collection at the Florence State Archive. As a Florentine diplomat Bartoli's primary responsibility would have been to inform Cosimo I regarding events in around Venice as well as occurring elsewhere and reported in Venice. A typically dense newsletter most likely emitted on 26 March 1568/9 (judging by the sequence of reports) bears news from Metz, Rome, Corfu, Vienna, Ancona, Antwerp and Strasbourg (called Argentina).[5] The Metz report, evidently based on a personal letter from which the names of sender and receiver have been removed, details the defeat of the Huguenots in the Battle of Jarnac during the Religious Wars. The report from Antwerp contains particularly hot news from the Spanish Netherlands, where the Duke of Alva has been sent by Spain to make sure the Index of Forbidden Books is being properly enforced in the version newly revised in 1564 in the context of the Council of Trent. It says, "all books" were "to be taken away from booksellers, merchants selling them, printers and whoever else, in order to examine them, and those which are not prohibited will be returned to the owners, and the others will be set aside to be burnt." The consequences from any such regulations, as will be explored in due course, were highly significant for printed news.

Not a scribe or a merchant or a diplomat but a retired courtier of English King Henry VIII, Petruccio Ubaldini supplies another name to the list of known newsletter writers. Having ended his career in the English court, he turns to Florentine Grand Duke Francesco I in 1575 perhaps hoping – suggests Anna Maria Crinò (1969) – to round out a meagre pension received from Queen

---

[5] ASF, MdP, vol. 3080, fols. 284r-288r.

Elizabeth but apparently receives no answer. He repeats his inquiry in 1579, this time by way of a letter to the Florentine resident in Paris, Sinolfo Saracini, accompanied by numerous newsletters dated from London, but the grand duke, informed of the offer, expresses disinterest in "that province," and there the matter rests. Finally in 1580, with Florentine curiosity about England on the increase, he finds an interested correspondent in Lorenzo Guicciardini, unofficial representative of the English court in Florence, who will receive the newsletters regularly until 1594.

A typical production by Ubaldini, dated London, September 26, 1579, begins with the queen. "After the departure of the Duke of Alanzone [Alençon]," he writes, "she went to take the air in different places not far" from the city of London.[6] At one of the homes belonging to her chamberlain, the Earl of Sussex, she was magnificently entertained with "jousts, tournaments, pole competitions, and hunts." At one of these last, "she too wanted to kill a deer by her own hand, always in the presence of the French ambassador." Another story takes us across the Irish Sea: "In Ireland after the death of that Gems Fimoris [James Fitzmaurice Fitzgerald], the Irishman, leader of the uprising of that country, who was killed by his own cousin, who in turn died in carrying out his plan, there is now the revolt of the Earl of Desmond his kinsman, as was supposed; and this one was against the Crown on other occasions." Indeed, "among the savages," that is, the indigenous population of Ireland, this Earl "possessed admiration and power as according to the custom of those places." Not to worry: there "will be a long and bothersome effort" but in the end the Crown would win. Concerning Scotland "at present there is nothing worth noting but peace and tranquillity."

In a few words the writer manages to express a particular political and cultural orientation, as was often the case in any given story. Native Irish people are bestial, justly subject to the civilizing process introduced by the English. The queen, he adds, with typical gender modelling, was an extraordinary woman – almost a man. In consideration of a possibly Catholic audience, religious issues are left out. In Bartoli's writings on the other hand an unabashedly Catholic viewpoint clearly stands out, and Huguenots, for instance, are portrayed as fanatical and unreliable, bent on destroying French society, while the actions of their opponents are most often seen in a positive light. Other newsletter writers, anonymous or not, fitted their accounts to the expected audience of their work (Kreuze 2023). Nonetheless, compilations deriving from several sources might carry the view of the various original writers, as when the Poles talked about "our" Polish troops deployed against

---

[6] ASF, MdP, vol. 4185, ff.nn.

the Muscovites in a newsletter by Bartoli, occasionally even risking contradiction with the views expressed in other news.[7]

A final example of a known Italian newsletter writer takes us into the realm of another sort of producer, frequenting the field of battle as well as the halls of state. Don Giovanni de' Medici, natural son of Grand Duke Cosimo I, was engaged from an early age in a wide range of activities on behalf of his family and Florence, including warfare, especially in the Low Countries (Dooley 2014, chaps. 1, 3). Back on the fields of Flanders around the time of the Siege of Ostend in the early years of the seventeenth century, he asks his older half-brother Grand Duke Ferdinando whether he might be allowed to send information not only to Florence but to Spain about what was going on, considering the interests involved. The response he receives touches upon most of the problems of undisguised authorship in such matters (Dooley 2026). Ferdinando admonished: "As for what Your Excellency mentions to me about wanting to send news to the Catholic Court about what is going on where you are, I have never thought this was a good idea, and the more I think about it the more I think this could be precisely a path to incite hatred and create difficulty and to always receive damage without any profit, and also run the risk of losing the personal favor of the Archduke and the Infanta [who are ruling Flanders]." Writings connected with the name and identity of the writer were necessarily placed under special scrutiny and could cause trouble in terms of reputation. "If Your Excellency writes frivolous things, this does not suit you; if you write things of great importance, and warn of what the Archduke would not want either written or told, His Highness will know immediately and there is cause for contention and malevolence."[8] The best solution was to avoid publicity and write only to his own ruler and court.

Giovanni, as if testing the extent of his independence, obeys the letter but not the spirit of the order (Dooley 2005). To ensure a constant supply of material to communicate to the grand duke, he enrolls friends and acquaintances, including field marshal Lodovico Melzi, in what could be called a veritable news bureau for producing the newsletters of Antwerp that now appear in the volumes of his correspondence in the hand of his secretary Cosimo Baroncelli. He explains the pattern of composition thus: "Your Highness will find the news about Ostende in the accompanying sheet, which is compiled from various letters that Cav. Melzi and other friends are constantly writing to me."[9] Ferdinando apparently allows this, and so the news continues throughout 1604. In his own dispatches to the Medici court, Don Giovanni simply paraphrases the newsletter he sends

---

[7] ASF, MdP, vol. 3079, fols. 507r-508-v.
[8] ASF, MdP vol. 5153, Insert 2, fol. 44v, 14 February 1603.
[9] ASF, MdP vol. 5157, fol. 99r, 23 April 1604.

accompanying his own letter, as shown below, just as ambassadors to various courts were now in the habit of doing. Who else might have received the now anonymous newsletter has not yet been discovered.

Don Giovanni dispatch:	Antwerp Newsletter:
As far as the news of these parts are concerned, I can only tell you that the enemy taking the opportunity of a fair that was being held in Arlon, in the country of Luxemburg, sent about 50 soldiers dressed as peasants, with good arms underneath, to take the portal of the town; and with four hundred horse entered and sacked everything, and besides taking the greatest booty ever taken in these parts, took as prisoners as about thirty of the principal townsmen who will pay the ransom for themselves and everyone else who remained.	The enemy, taking the opportunity of a fair that was being held in Arlon, in the country of Luxemburg, sent about 40 footsoldiers and horse dressed as peasants, and well armed underneath, who took the portal; and in an instant there appeared four hundred horse who entered and sacked whatever there was, and took as prisoners about thirty of the principal townsmen in the city and it was, so they say, the greatest booty ever taken in these parts. ASF, MdP, vol. 4256, November 18, 1604

Various figures have been identified as authors of the handwritten newsletters regularly acquired by Philipp Eduard of the Fugger family firm in Augsburg, Germany, and commonly called the Fuggerzeitungen. In Ausburg itself, for instance, there were Jeremias Crasser and Jeremias Schiffle. In Prague a certain Sebastian Westernacher was active in the period up until 1582 (Bauer 2011: 112 f). In the Venetian Fondaco dei Tedeschi, the commercial center frequented by German merchants, there were Michele Ciliano, Girarlo Bellinghen, and Arcate Arcangelo (Molino in Molino and Keller 2015: 110). Also in Venice a certain Hieronimus Acconzaioco was active and had this to say about news in general: "In all the conversations that people have with one another throughout the day, the conversations are increasingly about the latest news from all over the world, and even if they can sometimes be false, they nevertheless come across as so credible that one is inclined to trust their accuracy" (Molino in Molino and Keller 2015: 511).

Who wrote the typical Fuggerzeitungen story dated Antwerp, May 5, 1581, and now among the documents held in the Vienna State Archives, is still unknown, although a point of view is identifiable. "Eight days ago the soldiery and the Calvinists mutilated all the pictures and altars in the churches and cloisters of Belgium," begins the striking description here of a late episode in anti-Catholic iconoclasm (Klarwill 1924: 52). "The clergy and nearly five hundred Catholic citizens were driven out and several among them cast into prison," it adds. "Thus an end has been made of the Catholic Faith in Brussels, and Calvinism has been installed in its stead." There follows a subtle denunciation of the events, in consideration of the forced removal of traditional beliefs and the relevant symbols. "Since then, the masters of the guilds or brotherhoods, and the artisans, whose ancestors had founded several beautiful chapels and altars in the Church of our Dear Lady, have demanded that they themselves should be allowed to remove from the church the painted pictures and other ornaments. Upon the evening of the Feast of the Ascension they began to pull down the altars, occupied the churches and kept them locked until this day ... It is not known whether they will destroy everything within the church, but it is believed that it will come to pass here as it did in Brussels ..." Ultimately, in a somewhat ecumenical aside, the writer points to the practical consequences, noting that "as Catholics and Calvinists cannot keep peace with the Lutherans and Anabapists it will ill serve the promotion of commerce and many persons will leave this town."

Newsletter writers were active in London at least from the late sixteenth century, and by the early 1600s among the best known was John Pory. Author, traveler, and politician, he served as a member of Parliament from 1605 to 1610, where his practices gained sufficient notoriety for him to figure among the objects of a 1606 scurrilous poem, although he is perhaps best regarded for his role in the early colony of Virginia. Pory's clients, according to work by Sabrina Baron (2001: 55, 2010), included: Sir Robert Cotton, Sir Dudley Carleton (viscount Dorchester), John Chamberlain (the earl of Newport), Sir Thomas Puckering, Sir Thomas Lucy, Lord Brooke, Reverend Joseph Mead, George Garrard, persons in Virginia, and possibly Thomas Wentworth, the earl of Strafford. Few examples of the writings are extant, according to the biography by William S. Powell (1977), due in some cases to explicit instructions by the writer to destroy the sheet after reading, and in other cases due to the vagaries of heritage conservation in the nineteenth century.

Pory's sheets often tended to resemble personal letters, with salutation and closing, but like other newsletters they were bought and sold and came out on a weekly basis. An example, received by Dudley Carleton, ambassador in The Hague, reported on the execution of Sir Walter Raleigh in London in 1618, following a disastrous expedition to the New World: "Walter Ralegh's death ... being a matter of such great importance and renown, it is fitting that all tongues and pens, both good and bad, should be employed about it" (Powell 1952). Pory takes care to remind the recipient about their personal connection: "This day week, therefore, as I was writing my last letter to your lordship … " Next he delves into the tragic case at hand: "Sir Walter Ralegh being summoned from the Tower to come to the Lords at Whitehall, was there informed by their lordships that it was His Majesty's pleasure he should die upon the old sentence, and therefore was instructed within three days to prepare himself." Without apparent comment or criticism, he informs about Raleigh's last wish to be beheaded rather than hung, a more dignified end, which is granted. In a final judicial proceeding, Raleigh asks to be exempted from punishment, considering that the tacit concession of fifteen long years of liberty after the original condemnation, including responsibility for an ambitious, though unsuccessful, colonization scheme, bore all the signs of an implicit pardon. The court disagrees, and the execution proceeds.

Diffused far and wide by legions of writers, anonymous and not, the new form of news, regularly on sale for relatively little money, or in exchange for gifts and favors, was hailed by some as deserving of a place among the great inventions of the century, in spite of widespread criticism. Secondo Lancellotti, writing in the early 1600s about the origins of what was by then a long-established practice, had this to say, in a work decrying those he termed the "today-haters." It was not true, he insisted, that the sheets were full of lies, as was often said. Indeed, "if there is ever something of opinion or uncertainty in one sheet, it is always either confirmed or rejected in the next one" (Lancellotti 1636). All things considered, "the idea of sending the news (avvisi) of the actions, especially of Princes, all over the World, and knowing what was happening in Rome, in France, in Spain, in Germany, and elsewhere without spending a penny (frullo), was exquisitely ingenious." To justify the confidence he placed in the newsletters overall as a means of communication he pointed to the collection of them which he had seen in the offices of the Duke of Urbino. "I began to respect them all the more when I saw what an honored place they had in the regard of that Most Serene Lord."

Authorities were not so easily convinced. The Venetian government, by nature secretive and protective about the circulation of anything regarding internal matters and state interests, was unsurprisingly in the vanguard of the opposition. A 1567 deliberation by the Council of Ten referred specifically to "news of the world" and "especially regarding the Turk," as something to be kept under strict control.[10] Five years later, in February of 1572, the same government body explicitly denounced the "many in this city who make a public profession of writing news, for which they are paid by various people."

---

[10] Venice, Archivio di Stato [=ASV], Consiglio dei X, Deliberazioni, Secrete, Reg.8, c.82r, 17 marzo 1567.

The reference to regularly distributed and relatively accessible anonymous handwritten newsletters was clear. From now on, the decision continues, "there will be no person who in the future dares to write news of any kind, even that which is discussed in the streets, to send it out, or to give it in the city to a person of any status, even if they were ambassadors, rectors, or other ministers of ours, nor to foreigners of whatever rank they are." The penalties were particularly severe, taking into account of course the specifics of the accused: "if suitable for the galleys," the culprit was to be "condemned to the oar with irons on his feet for five years," whereas, "if not suitable," they were to be "banned for ten years from this city of Venetia, and from the district, and from all the other cities, lands and places of ours."[11]

The papacy too soon took action. In March of the same year 1572, Pope Pius V published an Apostolic Constitution explicitly aimed at the "writers, propagators or scribes of the bulletins commonly called avvisi" [Contra scribentes, exemplantes et dictantes monito vulgo dicta gli Avisi] (Bullarum 1826–84: 7, 969). The complaint derived from a deeply traditional notion of human affairs as lacking any intrinsic value in respect to the soul's salvation. In September a new Pope, Gregory XIII reinforced the same prohibition with the constitution "Against the slanderers known as news reporters, and those who receive their writings [Contra famigeratores nuncupatos menantes, et eorum scriptos recipientes]" (Bullarum 1826–84: 8, 12). There had emerged, he proclaimed, in fact, "a new sect" of "illicitly curious men." The evil intentions of such men was to "propose, collect, and write every piece of news concerning public and private affairs, of which they come to know or which through their malice they invent, regarding their own country and abroad." Worse yet, the proclamation went on, they mixed the true the false and the uncertain "without any restraint." The diffusion of such documents raised serious concerns, according to the Pope, as most of the purveyors "even for a base profit, send this news gathered from the voices of the people here and there, after making small summaries and without the name of the writer … " As a remedy the pope would "forbid anyone from daring to compile such summaries in the future, or seeking to receive, copy, disseminate or send those composed by others…" Punishments were to be determined by the case in question, but arrest, torture, imprisonment and possibly execution were to be expected. By 1590, ecclesiastics were being told to avoid even discussing "avvisi" in their sermons (Visceglia 2015: 758 n).

Court records demonstrate the zeal of the authorities, as well as the breadth and depth of the phenomenon. Indeed, when not from the chance inclusion of

---

[11] ASV, Consiglio dei X, Deliberazioni, Comuni, Reg.30, c.86v, 8 febbraio 1572.

a newsletter in the same archival folder as the news writer's diplomatic correspondence, many such writers have come to our attention in court records due to their trouble with the law. In Rome during the papacies of Pius V and Gregory XIII a certain priest named Annibale Cappello began frequenting the areas around the entrance to the Vatican, along with numerous other newsletter writers (Giansante 1975). Hoping to utilize his acquaintance with and servitude to the Cardinal d'Este for protection, he gained a reputation for particularly incisive reporting, or, as the authorities apparently believed, scandalmongering. Unsavory reports about his activity seemingly reached the ears even of Mary Stuart (Queen of Scots), who complained to the Pope. As his position in Rome became more dangerous due to the frequent injunctions against information, he attempted to flee the city, but was caught in Della Rovere-controlled Pesaro, beyond the papal state. After a brief time in prison, he was tortured and hung.

For the most part, the new prohibitions were met, in the world of the producers, mostly with indifference, and even gave rise to some dark humor. There was a distinction to be made, insisted one writer, in a message to his patron, Cardinal Ferdinando de' Medici, between the small-time jobbers presumably targeted, and himself. "The new prohibition against writing is all the more important and it increases my courage in serving you," he began, "as I am sure [the official document] is talking only about certain low-class newsletter writers who, having nothing else to do, foolishly take up talking about this and that prince."[12] Such was obviously not his practice. Indeed, because of this distinction he could hope for better treatment if worse came to worst. "I am sure that if I am sentenced to the galleys for this cause, Your Most Illustrious Lordship will ask the Pope to have me placed in the Capitana [the galley] of the Grand Duke [of Tuscany], where I have heard the slaves get to eat soup." The rest of the communication consisted of a typical newsletter beginning with a report from Brussels dated August 31, 1572.

Considering the importance of the genre and the frequent mentions in official documents, efforts from time to time have been made to assess the value of the information being communicated. Jean Delumeau (1957–9), for instance, defended the accuracy of newsletter data concerning the Roman grain supply. Ludwig Pastor, in his multivolume history of the papacy, makes widespread use of them when discussing the years of their greatest influence, for which they supply crucial information about the rumors circulating and conversations taking place around Rome, the opinions regarding particular foreign courts, and about the physical condition of the pope himself. True or false, they paint

---

[12] ASF, Miscellanea Medicea, vol. 29 insert 2, fol. 20r.

a highly variegated picture of the daily life in the largest cities of Europe, at both ends of the social and economic scale.

Not surprisingly, truth and falsehood were frequent themes in the newsletters themselves. A newsletter from Rome dated January 16, 1562, and now in the Florence State Archive [ASF] reported about a probably malicious story which causes a man to lose his life. We are told "that the people of Dieppe, hearing the first news concerning a victory obtained by the Huguenots, thinking that the rebels were victorious, killed the Captain of the land," but then, when the second news came, of the victory of the French King, "they declared themselves in favor of the said King, claiming that the captain had been killed because of some kind of grudge."[13] Queen Elizabeth I of England even gets involved, for on hearing of the pretended Huguenot victory, she immediately calls up an army of 3,000 to aid them at the front; and when the news is contradicted the whole plan gets put on hold.

A newsletter from the same place dated August 18, 1582, also in the ASF, carries yet another story about false news with significant consequences. In this case, the false news about a pardon, rather than encouraging leniency, had the opposite effect of hardening the pope's resolve, from his standpoint in order to not seem malleable to the nonsense being propagated in the news. "It was not true that the Pope [Gregory XIII] ordered [the prisoner, a certain] Neri not to be executed, as has been written, in return for 70,000 scudi," it begins.[14] "On the contrary, [Neri's] mother, sisters and some relatives went on Saturday to plead for mercy, weeping at the feet of the Pope, so that he would not let him die, but they did not succeed." No money was involved, it added. Nor were the family members alone in the pleading: "in the previous consistory, Cardinals Savello, Santa Croce and Maffeo" had made a similar request. The pope, rather than responding with compassion, decides that "denying this mercy was very important," because the news of a bribe was already in circulation, "and the honor of His Holiness as well as that of the Sacred College were at stake," so Neri is killed.

Among the newsworthy events that attracted widespread attention in newsletters all over Europe in the last decades of the sixteenth century was the sailing and eventual defeat of the Spanish Armada. Preparations for the attack on England had begun already in early 1587, but for various reasons things were delayed until the following year, amid constant miscommunications which can be traced from week to week within the newsletter material available to the grand ducal court in Florence. A report "from Spain" included in a newsletter dated March 26 announces that the Armada, with departure having been

---

[13] ASF, MdP, vol. 3079, fol. 192 v. [14] ASF, MdP, vol. 3083, fol. 313v.

scheduled for no later than the 20th of March, was not out to fight the English at all, but the Turks in northern Africa. Algeria, the writer remarked, was surely the destination; and the goal was to "carry out that enterprise so greatly desired by Christianity," of retaking the Ottoman lands.[15] For this reason it was thought that galleys were currently being prepared by the Turks in Constantinople in order "go to the defense of the ports of that realm." This defense would inevitably fail due to the efforts of "General Doria with help from the new galleys of the Pope, the Grand Duke, Savoy, Malta, Genoa, Naples, Sicily, and partly from Spain, which in all would form an armada of 80 very formidable galleys." In retrospect, such false news may even have been planted by Spanish counterintelligence.

The fleet finally set sail in July, but information was late and confused. A report from London contained in an Antwerp newsletter of September 3 says, "This evening there were letters from London dated the 29th of last month [i.e., August], with news that the Catholic Armada had arrived in Scotland, at an island called Hylandia in the Orkneys," possibly a corruption of the word "Highlands," which is not an island, although there is an Orkney island called Hoy.[16] In the sea battle, the English fleet captained by Francis Drake and Charles Lord Howard of Effingham had suffered significant losses, it was said. From Scotland, there was reliable information "that the people gave provisions and refreshments to the men," against royal policy, "and that when the king [i.e., James VI of Scotland] heard about this he decreed capital punishment for whoever gave them anything." Here again, the event in hindsight seems to be as fictitious as the place. A newsletter from Lyon dated the 6th of September brought the misleading story to a close: Drake was a prisoner and peace had been declared.[17]

More certain confirmation took days and weeks to prevail in the mediatic spiral. After a few engagements in the first days of August, amid bad weather and miscommunications with the Duke of Parma about ferrying troops out to meet the ships, and Drake in hot pursuit, the Armada finally ran up the Channel and along the Scottish coast, eventually circling around and down past Ireland. A Roman newsletter dated October 29, 1588, bearing a report about events that occurred in August and September, may be the most accurate. "From Midelburg [Middelburg] with letters of the 13th of this month they say that an English vessel had ... given news that 14 ships of the Armada had been sunk south of Ireland, with 600 Spaniards luckily being saved ... by an Irish gentleman, who was in disgrace with the Queen of England [Elizabeth I] ... hoping to have them

---

[15] ASF, MdP, vol. 3085, fol. 589r.   [16] ASF, MdP, vol. 3085, fol. 669r.
[17] ASF, MdP, vol. 4851, fol. 101r.

sent to England; and others say that many of the Spaniards were killed on the spot."[18] The newsletter goes on: Genoese merchants at Dunkirk, it says, have claimed that the ships were entirely broken up and dispersed by bad weather. "The Duke of Medina Sidonia arrived at the port of S. Andres [Santander] in Viscaya with just 25 ships," it says, "and 12 others [arrived] in Galicia at the port of La Coruña in very bad condition.

Accusations of inaccuracy in reporting were apparently well justified, but equally well-justified was the common assumption that the more scrupulous news writers corrected incorrect reports in a subsequent issue of the same newsletter. For instance, in a newsletter from Vienna, dated August 11, 1564, concerning a battle between the Muscovites and the Poles, we read, that "It was not true" that such a battle had taken place; nor was it true that "they then made a truce, as had been said."[19] Instead, it was found that the Muscovites "are still in the field with 50,000 horse, and are besieging Poloschi," and that the Poles had "a large army no more than 18 leagues away, so that they can easily come to blows" Another case of corrected news occurs in a newsletter from Naples bearing a story dated August 13, 1575, which states that "What was said of Uschiali [Ali Uluc] who was in Negroponte [Euboea] and with 120 galleys was not true, indeed today there is a notice from Constantinople [Istanbul] on the 13th that not a single galley was being armed nor would more than 50 be armed this year for the guards."[20]

As a means of self-protection, writers resorted to language admitting that sources might be unreliable; indeed sometimes this in itself could be the topic. For instance we have, in a newsletter from Milan dated November 3, 1574, a report from Turin stating that "Last week there were rumors in this city, and it was publicly said that the Grand Prior of France [Henri d'Angoulême] had arrived in Turin together with a commissioner sent by the Most Christian King to give back to the Duke of Savoy the forts the [king] now holds in Piedmont."[21] The writer adds, "but it was not subsequently verified, and although it is written that he is expected to come any day now, there is nonetheless no certain news about this, and this has given rise to the conclusion that some accident may have occurred, and that this restitution would not take place so quickly."

By acknowledging the presence and impact of rumor in their reports, early modern news writers provided precious evidence regarding the functioning of early modern cities as information echo chambers where the resonance eventually reached practically every level of society. For undertaking a linguistic account of the newsletter phenomenon as a whole as well as testimonies

---

[18] ASF, MdP, vol. 3085, fols. 674v, 675r.   [19] ASF, MdP, vol. 4572, fol. 261v.
[20] ASF, MdP, vol. 3082, fol. 300r.   [21] ASF, MdP, vol. 3254, fol. 108r.

regarding the question at hand, the EURONEWS Project transcribed thousands of newsletters from the Medici collection in the Florence State Archive, perhaps the most voluminous collection discovered to date, and marked them up for study.[22] Among the many relevant expressions and variants on the theme of rumor within a corpus of 1,088,099 words from newsletters written from 1550 through 1650 were found the following (Table 1).

The repetition of similar expressions on a regular basis adds a further dimension to the urban world currently being revealed in recent contributions on Venetian news by Filippo De Vivo (2007), on rumors more in general and fear in the Atlantic context in the collection by Hennington and Roper (2016), and on the gender dimension by Bernard Capp (2003) and Keith Botelho (2009).

To be sure, analyzing newsletter content with a view to understanding the news environment of those who read or in some way heard about these sheets is a time- and resource-consuming endeavor, begun on a massive scale only in the past twenty years. Among the largest bodies of relevant material located in a single archive, and therefore relatively accessible for large-scale analysis, is the collection of so-called Fuggerzeitungen at the Austrian National Library in

Table 1 Expressions indicating rumors, found in the EURONEWS Project database

it is said	*si dice*	the rumor heats up	*si riscalda la voce*
a rumor is circulating	*corre (la) voce*	the rumor is found	*si ritrova la voce*
a rumor is spreading	*sparso(a) voce*	the rumor persists	*persevera la voce*
a public rumor is spreading	*sparsa publica voce*	a rumor came out	*è uscita voce*
a certain rumor	*una certa voce*	it was rumored	*Andò voce*
a rumor is running around	*ruota voce*	the rumor was renewed	*Si rinova la voce*
a rumor continues	*continuandosi voce*	there being a rumor	*(es)sendo voce,*
the rumor has returned	*ri(re)novando la voce*	a single voice	*una voce sola*

---

[22] https://euronewsproject.org.

Vienna, covering the period from 1568 to 1605. Long regarded as relevant mostly from the standpoint of the interstate business interests of the wealthy Fugger family, the collection provides instead a vast panorama of handwritten newsletters as a whole.

In the first in-depth study of this material, Oswald Bauer (2011) demonstrated that commercial concerns, while present, for the most part take a notable back seat compared with stories about power and warfare. For understanding the contents in general, Bauer chose a sample of Fuggerzeitungen material from four months (March, June, September, December) out of each of the years 1569, 1572, 1578, 1588, and 1596. For analyzing this sample he devised a number of subject categories, defined in Table 2, acknowledging the caveats we often find throughout the methodological literature regarding possible distortions due to subjectivity.

Table 2 Fuggerzeitungen categories of analysis based on Oswald Bauer (2011)

War and violence 51%	Armaments, warfare, fighting, war economy (including troop supplies, financing war, paying soldiers, looting, confiscation of goods and piracy to the detriment of the opposing war party, paying for soldiers, fortresses or fleet construction) and defense, as well as displacement and suffering of the civilian population through the fighting.
Politics 25%	Negotiations and treaties between rulers, coalitions and alliances, embassies and audiences of ambassadors. In addition, decision-making bodies, assemblies of estates, meetings of council bodies as well as news about deaths of princes and politicians.
Economy 6%	Manorial finances, information about business activity and product prices, tax collection and authorization (unless explicitly levied for wars), minting and transporting money, princely finances, tributes, and the awarding of ecclesiastical benefices.
Society and culture 6%	Economic events as well as reports on journeys or descriptions of cities, news about people of note as well as personal letters and messages. In addition, social events such as festivals, weddings, and funerals.
Lawmaking and enforcement 4%	Reports on executions, trials, laws, and decrees, as well as reports on crimes.

Table 2 (cont.)

Religion 3%	Church festivals, scholars' disputes or debates, and reports where the religious aspect is presented as more important than the political; as well as canon law and the Inquisition.
Post/ communication 2%	Postal system, courier services and novelties, reports on (prints, etc.) as well as news about news
Nature/weather 1%	Natural disasters, severe weather of any kind (earthquakes, floods, droughts), but also fires, storms, diseases, epidemics and the weather in general.
Curiosities 1%	Miracles, healings, appearances in the heavens (e.g., comets) and oddities
Misc 1%	Everything else

Next to each category in the table we have placed the percentage of the whole, demonstrating the clear precedence of military and political matters, at 51 percent and 25 percent respectively.

Change over time in terms of subject matter according to Bauer's calculations is minimal in his Fuggerzeitungen corpus, with a few noteworthy exceptions. The year 1578 for instance shows a spike in values in the category of war and violence, due presumably to the continuing struggles in the Low Countries and the expedition to North Africa that year by the Portuguese king. Likewise 1596 shows an uptick due to an intensification in the ongoing war against the Ottomans as well as a number of significant single successes by the imperial troops such as the capture of the fortress of Hatvan, offset by the Turkish victory over the Imperial troops in the Battle of Keresztes. The relative importance of news about culture and society is also striking in the first three years surveyed (1569, 1572, and 1578), compared to 1588 and 1596. This depends in particular, at least in the first two years under study, on the particular interest of Philipp Eduard Fugger in news about social events, notes Bauer. "Law" on the other hand plays a major role in 1569 probably due to the fact that in many of the communications that year princely mandates were included in their entirety. Finally, looking at the whole corpus, in the months of December and March, reports of violence and war fall below the 50 percent mark, most probably due to the seasonal dynamics, with reports of policy on the increase, whereas the opposite takes place in the military campaign months of June and September.

Confirming the collection's integration into a far wider network of information exchange, copies of items among the Fuggerzeitung material can be found in other archives such as the Mediceo del Principato collection in the Florence State Archive (Molino 2015). For instance, in both places we find the same story, dated July 1575, with basically the same wording, to the following effect: "The Pope [Gregorius XIII] has granted to Cardinal Guastavillano [Filippo Guastavillano] the *spolia* of the Bishop of Faenza [Giovanni Battista Sighicelli] in the amount of 8 thousand scudi." And yet another, from November of the same year, in both archives, says: "they say that the King [Rudolf II von Habsburg] will be sent to Potsdam to the Diet where it is also said, but not believed, that His Caesarian Majesty [Maximilian II von Habsburg] will be present and it is rumoured that the imperial Diet will be sooner than has been written." Other examples abound.

Based on the Medici papers in the Florence State Archive for the year 1600, a study by the EURONEWS Project team attempted to give an idea of the topical breadth of the relevant items in a single time segment (Mansutti et al. 2024). The 96 newsletters belonging to that year originated from all over Europe, with especially frequent issues from Antwerp, Cologne, Milan, Genoa, and Graz, and the rest from Ostend, Prague, Paris, Brussels, Vienna, Lyon, Turin, Venice, Rome and Madrid. Study of the contents was organized around the five major themes of power, commerce, regions, diffusion, and rhetoric. Necessarily, there were matters in the life of those times that appeared in the sources rarely or not at all, just as there were transversal subthemes that crossed all categories and required treatment in each, such as, for instance, religion, disease, natural disaster, gender, family, and society.

References to the exercise of power, arguably the main material of news, not surprisingly, were particularly prominent in 1600. Indeed, the first ten items in a frequency table of the most-used words were mainly about this. Personages whose actions are worth recounting, according to the norms holding sway in those years, belong to, or stand close to, courts or various sorts of governing bodies or ecclesiastical institutions capable of turning actions into events and events into news. Table 3 shows the raw frequency of the first ten terms, along with the number of documents in which the term occurs.

The main stories on this subject generally revolve around war, internal affairs (including law and order), diplomacy and negotiations, courts and officials, hence the relative frequency of terms like "lord," "duke" and "majesty." Recurring themes include the middle stages of the Eighty Years' War between the United Netherlands and its allies on the one side and the Spanish Empire and its allies on the other. The conflict between France and the Duchy of Savoy over control of the Marquisate of Saluzzo continues. Meanwhile, the long Turkish

Table 3 EURONEWS Project figures on the ten most frequent terms in 1600

Term		Freq	Docs	Term		Frq	Docs
lord	signor	134	82	part	parte	84	56
duke	duca	112	81	letters	lettere	84	64
majesty	maestà	93	72	count	conte	78	61
thousand	mila	93	61	king	re	73	52
highness	altezza	89	60	peace	pace	73	55

war between the Habsburg Monarchy and the Ottoman Empire continues. Diplomacy, when it exists, often deals with one of these three issues. Internal affairs include the punishment of crimes and the regulation of religious life. Ceremony is similarly circumscribed and localized, and aims to create respect and loyalty for appointed authorities in church and state.

A particularly important engagement in the ongoing Eighty Years' War was the battle of Nieuwpoort with Archduke Albert of Flanders on the Spanish side fighting against Maurice of Nassau leading the Dutch. Here is the first account in the documents, of the events of the 2nd of July:

> On the second of July His Highness left Bruges to go and follow the said Prince Maurice, who was said to have gone toward Ostend and Nieuwpoort, and to have turned ... as though going toward Dunkirk, hoping to fight him with good hopes of putting him to flight, but this did not happen, because His Highness having caught up with the said Prince between Nieuwpoort Castle and Ostend, although at first [His Highness] had the advantage, and practically destroyed the enemy's rearguard, nonetheless attempting to engage, [he] ran into the battle which had stalled, and having thrust forward with his cavalry followed by many thousands of mutineers, the said cavalry reversed itself on the mutineers, and the mutineers reversed onto the rest of the infantry, so the whole army was put to flight and then was so hotly pursued by the said Prince Maurice that most were cut to pieces, and His Highness was forced to retreat to Bruges with three horses and then to Ghent, where he now is. The battle was very bloody due to the lengthy combat, and they say ten thousand men were killed on both sides. His Highness was slightly injured in two places on his face. The admiral of Aragon was killed; the Duke of Umala was injured, and all his retinue including the pages was killed; don Luigi di Velasco, the Count of Berleymont, and La Barlotta were saved. His Highness lost all his weapons and baggage, along with all his retinue.[23]

The breathless momentum of the narrative seems to emphasize the rapid developments described and possibly first reported by an eyewitness to the

---

[23] ASFI, MdP, 4256, fol. 43r.

events. Soon there would be the Siege of Ostend, one of the most discussed events of the war (Thomas 2020). The style of delivery may bear a resemblance to the widely heard oral accounts, of which the "wars in ottava rima," referring to particularly interesting battles, were a notorious popular tradition in Italian streets and squares in the previous century and probably even later (Rospocher 2017). The presence of a troop of soldiers ("mutineers") who had mutinied at the town of Diest the year before due to unfavorable conditions, but grudgingly agreed to continue on the Spanish side after agreements about interim payments, adds a further element of uncertainty (Parker 1973: 42). In closing, the author assumes that events will unfold according to plan, but at the same time sows the seed of doubt by suggesting that "Further details are not known with certainty, but we will be informed in two days, and I will report." Whether he kept his word is not known.

Such accounts of major battles often contain precious clues about military history worth comparing to current scholarship. Just around the time of the action, a new technique was reportedly being tried and tested, involving the use of infantry volleys, in which ranks of soldiers fired simultaneously and then fell back while another rank took their place. First supposed to have been used at Nieuwpoort in July 1600 (Parker 2007), such a practice may be what our author intends by saying that parts of the army fell back on the ranks behind them – for example, the "mutineers" on the rest of the infantry. Whether this specific practice is indeed the case here, or whether we are simply in the presence of a refinement in military discipline (Sicilia Cardona 2013), we leave the question open.

In the documents from 1600, religion appears in the context of the spread of Christianity through the planned founding of a church in Peru, for example: "Yesterday morning a long consistory took place in which Cardinal Deza, after the audiences, proposed a church in the Indies of Peru ... "[24] The same line continues with "Cardinal d'Ossat proposed a monastery in France ... " reminding about the continued importance of missionary work within European Christianity. Elsewhere, readers were also warned when beliefs or structures were threatened. The impact of the French Wars of Religion was still being strongly felt, despite the Edict of Nantes and the Peace of Vervins in 1598, and the corresponding events became news. Likewise, struggles against Ottoman expansion in southeastern Europe occasionally took on the character of a crusade, with the Holy Roman Emperor assuming, at least in principle, the role of defender of the faith (Vocelka 1985). Confessional disputes and internal conflicts, as considered here, speak more to the political significance of religion

---

[24] ASFI, MdP, vol. 4028, fols. 7v-8r.

and its power as an instrument of order than to its essential influence on consciousness. In the world described, other literary genres were better suited to deal with the latter. Nevertheless, these reports seem to confirm their reputation for being effective in conveying the excitement and dismay week after week, month after month, over the unfolding disaster.

In spite of the criticism, the handwritten newsletters were always of interest, and for this reason alone they illuminate an important corner of the early modern episteme. Defying the physical limitations on the reproduction potential of handwritten sheets, they came to play an important role in every major commercial enterprise and court. Furthermore they bear witness to an increasingly widespread awareness of the wider world beyond the visible horizon, agitated by the ever-present element of change that may be taken as a characteristic of news per se: in the news, for better or for worse, there was (and is, we might add) almost always something to get excited about. But soon the advantages of regular news were to inspire an altogether new publication type, with enormous consequences, as we shall see.

4 News in Print

Three years after the fall of Constantinople, in 1456, an urgent message circulated throughout Europe, insisting that Mehmed II, the Ottoman sultan, had "conceived in his mind to destroy the entire Christian population and the Western Empire, becoming ever more prepared each day to invade it violently" (Baronius [1588-1607] 1880: 67). Shocking news, to be sure. The author, Pope Callixtus III (Alonso de Borja), proclaimed his commitment "to oppose, to the best of our ability, these so pernicious forces with our own strength and that of the Roman Church." The communication, which came to be known by the words in the first line, *Cum his superioribus annis* ("In these past years"), was addressed to the "patriarchs, archbishops, bishops" as well as "ecclesiastical personages everywhere in the Christian world," bearing precise orders regarding prayers and processions and other observances among the rest of the faithful, to be accompanied by a renewed call to arms. This was an emergency (such was the meaning), and something had to be done.

A previous call for a crusade, just after the Turkish victory of 1453, had seemingly fallen on deaf ears, in spite of distribution throughout the same capillary network that bound and informed people of the church, and those who listened to them, across the known world since the Middle Ages (Runciman 1965: 165). This time was different, however. A new device was available to ensure that even deaf ears might be opened, that even those who did not go to church might see in writing what was said. Johannes Gutenberg in

Mainz had perfected the first printing press, and by this means, around the same time as the completion of the 42-line bible, the best-known production of these years (Bechtel 1992: 265), he printed copies of the papal message in Latin and German, the latter versions being known as "Die Bulla widder die Turcken" (The Bull against the Turks).

As it happened, the pope's new crusade never materialized due in part to disinterest among the major European powers. Gutenberg went out of business due in part to the costs of printing the bible. Meanwhile, printing gradually assumed an informational as well as religious role all over Europe. Print shops emerged in Cologne (1464), Basel (1468) Augsburg (1468), and Nuremberg (1470) and very soon in numerous other geographical and linguistic areas: Paris in 1470, Venice in 1469, followed by Ferrara, Florence, Milan, Bologna, and Naples in 1471; Lyon and the Low Countries got presses in 1473, London in 1476, Segovia in 1472, then Valencia, Zaragoza, Barcelona, and Seville, and even Mexico City in 1539. In terms of productivity, Venice took an early lead in the first half-century and continued to dominate as an interregional center in Italy along with Rome and Milan, whereas Paris, the Low Countries and the German cities took over an ever greater share over the course of the sixteenth century. The reasons for these transformations have long been matters for debate among print historians (Richardson 1999). The availability of the online tools and data provided by the Universal Short Title Catalogue currently being developed at the University of St Andrews [=USTC] renders obsolete most prior attempts at forming a statistical picture.

Alongside massive editorial projects involving works for long-term use, study and enjoyment, early printing poured out a steadily increasing stream of ephemera. Designed for the moment, these conveyed, like the papal message we have been examining but without the conservation value of the pope's own words, the latest news along with essential information demanding immediate attention. Eminently disposable once the moment had passed, they were particularly vulnerable to the ravages of time. Many which have left no trace are assumed to have disappeared into the vast "legion of the lost" that print historians estimate to include far more titles than our libraries, bibliographies, or virtual inventories have ever recorded.

Apart from papal bulls, letters, indulgences for specific causes, and state or city ordinances, there were news pamphlets of all kinds and lengths, many of them designed to be produced in the course of a single day (Pettegree 2010: 135). An example was the 8-page 1482 *Nachricht von den Türken* ("Report on the Turk") published in Memmingen by Albrecht Kunne (USTC No. 746203). In Germany many bore "Zeitung" or "Neue Zeitung" in the title, signifying "timely report," long before the term came to be applied to the new printed newspapers. In addition, titles might include enough information to serve as advertisements in themselves. For instance, the 4-page 1510 "Timely Report [Neue Zeitung] about the peace negotiations between His Papal Holiness and the king of France mediated by the orator of His Imperial Majesty the King of Spain and England" published in Nuremberg by Johann Weißenburger in 1510 (USTC No. 677019).

But the boom in paper-borne reproductions involved not only the products of the letter-press. News-bearing items at the dawn of printing, broadly conceived in terms of reproduction techniques, included also single-sheet woodcuts, or, increasingly, copper plate engravings, bearing almost self-explanatory nontextual information about current events, run off in numerous copies. Military actions were particularly susceptible to such a visual approach (Lamal 2023: 92). Because of the meticulousness of the preparation, a month could pass from event to publication in the case, for example, of the multiple depictions of contemporary battles and sieges produced by the Antwerp painter and printmaker Hieronymus Cock. But considering the challenges of timeliness, readers no doubt felt informed by the prints from his workshop, including, according to the study by P. Martens (2024), military engagements at Boulogne, 1549; Mahdia, 1550; Mirandola, 1551; Parma, 1551; Thérouanne, 1553, in two different prints, one lost; Hesdin, 1553; Renty, 1554, lost; Siena, 1555; Ostia, 1556; Saint-Quentin, 1557; Gravelines, 1558, lost; Centallo, 1558; and Malta, 1565. The depiction of Centallo in Piedmont, for instance, showed the fortified town itself with its walls and four bastions, under siege on behalf of King Philip II of Spain by the Duke of Sessa, whose troops are shown marching in formation in one area, and in another, firing cannon behind makeshift dunes and bulwarks.

A particularly rich series of illustrations evidently intended to accompany or indeed substitute for verbalization about warfare was produced by various artists and entrepreneurs in Geneva between 1569 and 1570 and published as "Forty tableaux or divers memorable histories concerning the wars, massacres and troubles that have occurred in France in these last years." As a guarantee of accuracy the title added the attestation that "all material was gathered from the testimony of those who were there in person and saw them, and truly portrayed." Depictions included the Massacres of Cahors, Vassy, Sens, and Tours; the Captures of Valence and Montbrison; and the Battles of St Gilles and Dreux. Scholarship on the period and production process has attempted to identify particular confessional or political positions; but in the last analysis, the effort to convey a sense of what actually happened appears to have been genuine, adding a further element to the development of news publication at the time (Benedict 2007).

An important innovation in the period, joining prior technology to the new world of movable type, was the incorporation of images, often executed in woodcut, into pages set in lead letters. This made for even more spectacular title pages to otherwise modest publications, such as for instance the four-page 1531 piece written by Jan Dantyszek and published in Antwerp with the title "The wonderful and triumphant victory of the most illustrious king of Poland against Count Hans Weida of Muldani," featuring a generic battle scene with two armies of cavalry and infantry clashing spectacularly, at the moment when lances impale bodies, and corpses lie dismembered on the ground (USTC No. 437548). Such generic images could be reused for repeated publications regarding other battles (Pettegree 2010: 147).

Not only wars and international affairs, but also local and regional tragedies such as murders, famines, earthquakes, floods, and the like might find eager audiences through such publications. In the realm of so-called "murder pamphlets" with an antiecclesiastical significance, consider a 1550 item in Italian but without place or printer, claiming to be a "Copy of a letter recently arrived from Ravenna, which contains the horrendous incident that occurred in Pigneta, Ravenna, of two friars from Ravenna, who killed a merchant to take from him four thousand and more ducats, with his capture and death," and featuring on the cover an illustration of a dying man lying in bed with two monks looking on while a third takes down notes, presumably about the fortune left by the deceased (Salzberg 2014: 138). Twenty-three years later, a pamphlet printed in London claimed to offer "A True Reporte" on a family drama (USTC No. 507616), where a man kills his wife, followed by neighborhood involvement in delivery and indictment of the criminal (Whipday 2024). Scandal and voyeurism no doubt added to the entertainment value of such informational items.

Broadsheets printed on one or both sides of a single sheet, the easiest and fastest product, have been indicated by press historians as highly mobile and highly saleable items that could fill a printer's coffers while weightier works were under way (Pettegree 2017). News-related sheets included for instance the one printed in Latin by Reutlingen printer Michael Greyff in 1480 and entitled "Here follow the miracles which through the mercy of God took place at the time of the siege of the city of Rhodes and the battles that took place then" (USTC No. 741185), including five particular occurrences that, in the view of the writer, confirmed the divine favor enjoyed by the inhabitants (Herzfeld 1972). Another from 1516, printed in Munich with woodcut figures by painter-printmaker Hans Burgkmair the Elder (Geisberg and Strauss 1974: 477) but listed as "Lost" in the USTC, was entitled "This child was born in Tettnang" (Disz künd ist geboren worden zu Tettnang). The illustration shows the infant sitting on a cushion with a foot growing out of its stomach, next to another view showing the same infant asleep holding the protruding foot. We are told, "On the eighth of April, in the year 1516 after the birth of Christ, in the half hour after the clock had rung once after midnight, a child such as you see above was born to the noble lord Ulrich Graue of Muntfort and the town of Tettnang by a woman named Anna Bingerin, wife of Conrad Miller" (Park and Daston 1998: 186). A brief description followed, taking in what was visible in the print: "When the child was awake its legs were apart and when it slept it held its little foot in its hand. And it was a little girl who lived nine days. The said lord and count called his artist, Master Matheysen Miller, citizen of Lindau, to draw or portray the child and ordered it printed, as is seen above." Thus the text emphasizes the truth value of the artist's involvement in the transmission of information, an important detail.

Spectacular natural phenomena were news and at the same time harbingers of good or ill fortune thus providing edifying occasions for prophecies about the future and commentaries on divine providence. A famous example was a broadsheet entitled "About the meteorite that fell before Ensisheim in the year 1492"[25] (Von dem Donnerstein gefallen im XCII Jahr vor Ensisheim), published in Basel by the Strasburg-based scholar Sebastian Brant, including an eye-catching illustration by an anonymous engraver showing a huge object falling from an angry sky before an awestruck crowd, and including a poem by Brant in Latin and German, explaining the significance for the current political conjuncture. In another example, Paulus Fabricius, mathematician to the Holy Roman Emperor, published a broadsheet concerning the comet of 1556 (USTC 752349), illustrated with an astronomical diagram presumably furnished by himself, showing the presumed path of this comet, all accompanied by a long discussion explaining how the comet "threatens war and pestilence," but was "much more directed towards secret treachery and especially betrayal." Reprintings by other printers were legion in the early years of the industry before regulatory systems were put in place.

Songs made good news media, often in broadside form (Roper 2017). Such broadside ballads were indeed the most economical song type related to news events, and instead of musical notation, they often included text references to popular melodies diffused by voice. Consider for instance, in regard to an event in the early sixteenth-century Italian wars, a 1525 publication (USTC 553967) entitled: "A beautiful news song about the recent battle of Pavia which took place on Matthew's Day [September 21st]," to be sung to the tune of "The Seven Soldiers," apparently in reference to a current popular song. Another musical

---

[25] Tubingen University Library, Shelfmark Ke XVIII 4 a.2 (Nr. 23).

broadsheet (USTC 553992) referred to the "Oudewater Massacre" during the Dutch Revolt, in which Spanish troops on August 7, 1575, subjected the town, situated between the provinces of Holland and Utrecht, to a brutal siege followed by a bloodbath, sacking, and partial demolition. In this case the item was entitled "Song about the siege and tragic death that occurred," specifying that the words were to be applied to the melody of "Oh God have mercy through Christ your Son."

Particular events might call forth a variety of such forms, with startling effects, as related by the Venetian patrician and diarist Girolamo Priuli, during the war of the League of Cambrai (1508–1516). The struggle saw Venice opposed by an array of powers including the Holy Roman Empire, Spain, and France, along with former Italian allies intent upon pushing back the maritime state's prior incursions into the Italian terraferma. Priuli was amazed at the output of real, fake, bizarre, and surprising news in all forms. "Throughout all of Italy, France and Germany there were made and described so many fables, blatherings, sonnets, songs, verses and then so many writings by learned people as well as the ignorant, in many modes and styles, concerning this ruining of the Venetian state" (Rospocher and Salzberg 2021: 7). The numbers were significant, though unknown, except by the evidently constant activity of the printers. "I could not say how many books and papers were written and filled with similar material and continuously even daily many were made and the printers had much to do to print such things and publicize not only throughout Italy but throughout the whole world the ruin of this poor Venetian State." Impact was obvious, if "throughout the streets and public places of the major cities of the world nothing was sung or sold by the usual charlatans except stories and verses and songs and other various things about this great Venetian disaster."

Shortly afterward, Martin Luther's break with Rome filled the news, and the precise role of the printed word in the Protestant Reformation is still a matter of debate (Rubin 2014). The ninety-five theses came out in October 1517 and immediately were picked up, the scholarship says, by three different publishers (Eisenstein 1979: 307). Months later Luther himself told Pope Leo X that "it is a mystery to me how my theses, more so than my other writings, indeed those of other professors, were spread to so many places. They were meant exclusively for our academic circle here..." (Eisenstein 1979: 306). Nonetheless, the Latin theses were immediately translated and printed in German and reached a wide audience, as did the subsequent publications, so that one estimate supposes that Luther's 30 publications between 1517 and 1520 sold 300,000 copies or more (Dickens 1968: 51).

The Reformation, it has been said, was at once a symptom of print development and a motor for the same; and in the years following Luther's break with

Rome, Reformation-related news reached fever pitch (Pettegree and Hall 2004). Invitations to side with one or another of the parties among the reformers themselves and among the various states and regions across the developing confessional fault lines filled printers' presses and the hands and eyes of an avid public, especially considering the value for souls as well as societies. Sermons not only gained widespread audiences but became news, emanating from all sides, to an extent still not possible to measure. The USTC lists more than 2,000 separate printed items in Europe designated as "sermon" (and cognates) in the years between 1520 and 1550.

But the Reformation did not spread through publication by words alone (Cressy 1989, Watt 1991, Pettegree 2005). A broadsheet illustration (Figure 4), exceptionally detailed though evidently aimed at wide distribution, encapsulated the essence of the movement's early phase. Entitled "On the Old

Figure 4 The Old and the New Belief (*Neudrucke Deutscher Litteraturwerke des XVI und XVII Jahrhunderts – Flugschriften aus der Reformationszeit*, vol. XII, Halle, 1896)

and the New God / Faith / and Teaching" ("Vom alten und nüen Gott/Glauben und Ler"), it came out in 1521, months after Luther burned the papal bull condemning his writings (Eire 1989: 75). The message was an open vendetta against papal power. Following the title, the image is divided vertically. On the left, a devilish long-beaked pope (the new "God" in the title), replete with sword in one hand and spurious key to Heaven in the other, is being informed on one side of the head by a crow and on the other by a tiny devil. He sits on a platform from which there protrude his human-looking leg and his other reptile-looking one, while all this is being held aloft by a cardinal, a canon and the Greek philosopher Aristotle (as labeled) – perhaps in reference to excess intellectualism as the enemy of virtue. Below these is a crowd of well-known anti-Luther polemicists, also labeled. On the right we have God the Father in heaven sending down his Son who, accompanied by the Holy Spirit, gives instruction to the evangelists and to Luther himself.

Which of these items, allowed to circulate more widely, might escape the attention of distracted officials where the effects could be disruptive was anybody's guess. Already in 1515, Pope Leo X at the Fifth Lateran Council lauded the printing press as an invention conceived "through divine goodness," while ordering measures to prevent possible dangers (Schroeder 1937: 504). Printing he pointed out, "has brought untold blessings to mankind" due to the affordances regarding "the study of the sciences" and the possibility that more individuals "may conveniently improve themselves," not to mention the usefulness for "the instruction of infidels" and for "strengthening the faith" of the faithful. Nevertheless, there had already been "attacks on persons holding positions of dignity and trust." The effects could be devastating. The reading of such things "is not only not conducive to the intellectual well-being of the reader but also leads to grave errors in matters of faith and morals, whence have arisen numerous scandals and daily greater ones are to be feared." He therefore requested the approval of the Council for a new system of controls. There would be pre-publication censorship of "any book or any other writing whatsoever." Every manuscript would be "carefully examined and its publication approved by our vicar and the Master of the Sacred Palace," and elsewhere in Italy and Christendom in general, "by the bishops or by competent persons appointed by them and by the inquisitor of the city or diocese in which the books are to be printed." It was a significant step with enormous consequences.

For more easily identifying and indicating, for purposes of public tranquility, what could and could not be bought or sold at home and abroad (Farge 1989), preliminary indices of forbidden books were drawn up in the first decades of the sixteenth century by the Sorbonne in Paris (1540) and by the Venetian government (1547). Pope Paul IV published an Index (1559) accompanied by instructions to local bishops and even private householders to examine printed matter in their midst for possible prohibited items to be eliminated. These efforts were soon followed by those of the Council of Trent (1564); and by the time of the foundation of the Congregation of the Index in 1572, most states' civil governments had allowed or deputed various combinations of churchmen, government representatives, and trade organizations to step in and require approval of manuscripts for publication while exercising oversight over book imports.

Indeed, with ideas as conveyed by the printing press having become symptoms and also triggers of actions in a period of conflict and consolidation at the religious and political levels, regulatory measures soon became the order of the day in both church and state, and in Roman Catholic as well as Protestant places. In 1559 Queen Elizabeth of England issued an Injunction condemning the "great disorder" that had arisen "by publication of unfruitful, vain, and infamous books and papers" (Prothero 1898: 169). Pre-publication censorship was the only remedy. Thus,

> no manner of person shall print any manner of book or paper of what sort, nature, or in what language soever it be, except the same be first licensed by her majesty by express words in writing, or by six of her Privy Council, or be perused and licensed by the Archbishops of Canterbury and York, the Bishop of London, the chancellors of both universities, the bishop being ordinary, and the archdeacon of the place where any such shall be printed, or by two of them whereby the ordinary of the place to be always one.

Making the process even more cumbersome, "the names of such that shall allow the same [are] to be added in the end of every such work for a testimony of the allowance thereof." Even in the fledgling Dutch Republic, in spite of the later-conceived reputation for relative indifference, there were severe punishments for publishers, writers, and sellers of works critical of religion or politics. In 1580 William of Orange signed a proclamation requiring pre-publication censorship by representatives of the States of Holland, repeated in 1584 (Harline 1987: 128).

As the century wore on, the disruptive potential of print came to be articulated in the starkest terms by the strongest defenders, which could be taken as a warning to friend and foe alike. The Italian scholar Tommaso Garzoni proclaimed, in his *Universal Marketplace of All Professions in the World* (Venice: Somascho, 1585: 847), that printing was "truly a rare stupendous and miraculous art." By it, he claimed, "we are able to tell gold from lead, the rose from the thorns, the wheat from the chaff; we are made acquainted with the good as well as with the bad." Now we know the learned and we know the ignorant and all the world can see the difference. "The darkness of ignorance is all gone. No more can lies be passed off as truths nor black be made to seem white." Social divides were called into question, if "everyone may give judgement concerning an infinite number of things about which, without printing, they would be unable to open their mouths to speak, much less judge." Not the printer, but the mighty should beware, he warned.

> This is the art that indicates the fools, that exposes the arrogant, that makes known those who are learned ... This is the art that gives fame to honourable persons, that scorns and vituperates the vicious, that buries dead brains in the depths of the earth, that exalts lively and sublime minds to the heavens. This is the art that is the mother of honours to the worthy and the house of shame to the unworthy.

In response to such ideas, from the authorities' point of view, there was only one possible conclusion: repression.

The effect of the new regulatory climate no doubt complicated the production and circulation of printed material, but did little to dampen the enthusiasm among readers. Each new press rule provoked authors, printers, publishers, and purchasers to conceive of new strategies of evasion. Material destined for more tightly controlled markets was shipped via the free ports or smuggled across state lines in shipments of other sorts of merchandise. Few dared to suggest, with the early seventeenth-century Italian polemicist Ferrante Pallavicino (1618–1644), that censorship brought publicity; but no one could deny that the demand for certain works, including those conveying news, was inevitably enhanced by official sanctions. Meanwhile, officials in church and state soon began to recognize the potential of the press for ideological purposes – their own and others'.

In spite of the uncertainties, well into the sixteenth century and beyond, throughout the print world, numerous occurrences appear to take on the character of media events by the combination of widely distributed printed material, informative or propagandistic or both (Ettinghausen 2016). Examples included the Peace of Cateau-Cambresis of 1559, ending the Italian Wars; and the iconoclastic attacks in the Low Countries in 1566 followed by the revolt against Spain. The victory of Christian forces against the Ottoman Turks at the Battle of Lepanto in 1572 was accompanied, like these other events, by a varied assortment of material, printed and manuscript, long before becoming visually and pictorially memorialized, in this last case by Paolo Veronese on the walls of the Sala del Collegio in the ducal palace in Venice. Regulators could hardly keep up; and in certain cases could be imagined to be devoting most attention to particularly odious material, with much of the rest allowed to slip through.

Consider the way news from England regarding the execution of Mary Queen of Scots in February 1587 by order of Elizabeth I echoed throughout Europe, with special intensity in France, as recorded by the diarist Pierre de l'Estoile (Wilkinson 2004: 103). Mary's French connection, including the late royal spouse, Francis II, was particularly significant in the context of the ongoing religious wars. Says l'Estoile, after a grisly secondhand account of the execution, "the satires, placards, commemorations and speeches on this death, flew to Paris and everywhere, and were disseminated there according to the affections and passion of the parties." This he follows with twelve examples, mostly transcribed in their entirety, including critical verses, a funeral poem, and a dialogue between a Frenchman detesting the execution, and an Englishman supporting it, taken from a letter to the diarist's friend, with the comment that the event was "the topic of most of the talk of idle groups."[26] According to other scholarship, the echo of the execution event in Spain and the Spanish court was such as to help inspire Philip II's plan for an Armada to invade England (Mattingly 1959: 17).

Recent work on the way news circulated in Germany regarding the War of Cologne (1582-90) suggests important ramifications in the light of scholarship on early modern publicity. The war occurred after the prince-elector and archbishop of Cologne Gebhard Truchsess joined the Protestant confession, intending to marry and keep his title with the associated incomes. The decision delegitimized the Cologne government and instantly created a Protestant majority among the Imperial electors, raising the specter of a non-Catholic emperor at some future time. The ensuing war, which eventually became mixed up in the hostilities between Spain and Holland, was accompanied by a war of words. Eve-Marie Schnurr (2009), analyzing the 182 surviving German-language texts, shows how the pamphlets, poetry, trade fair reports and news sheets discussed Truchsess' confessional switch, the petition by the Cologne Protestants to the Emperor, and the events of the war, while debating such basic principles as religious freedom, "German liberty," and duty to God, Church, and state. Combining qualitative with quantitative content analysis, she shows the relative importance of discussions of legitimacy over simple information (drawing here on Uwe Jochum), of emotional appeals over appeals to reason (referring to Miriam Chrisman), while identifying such attitude-building elements as demonizaton of the enemy (p. 388), charges of "tyranny" (p. 392), references to the Spanish "black legend" (p. 391). The more analytical writings, tending to reach into the political decision-making process and the

---

[26] L'Estoile P. de (1876) *Mémoires Journaux de Pierre de L'Estoile*, ed. M. Brunet, A. Champoillon, E. Halphen, P. LaCroix, C. Reid, T. de Larroque & E. Tricotel. t. III. Paris: Lemerre, 139.

cabinets of princes, she finds, are more prominent where the object of attack is weaker – in this particular case, the Protestant side (p. 403).

Was there a public sphere in late sixteenth-century Germany or elsewhere, of individuals discussing political matters in public on a regular basis in opposition or in juxtaposition to the ruling authorities? Because of the emancipatory implications of the concept as introduced by Habermas, Schnurr (2009) joins Wolfgang Behringer (2006) in opting for a notion closer to Manuel Castells' "Space of Flows," where critical discussion was first made possible. Other research suggests that restricted or ad hoc public spheres may have existed here and elsewhere at various times in response to particular events, while a more permanent version may have emerged during the religious wars in France and the revolt of the Netherlands (Briggs and Burke 2009, chap. 3). Reaching further into the present, the original author has modified the concept to include the ongoing destruction of the wider public sphere by the formation of micro-publics in the age of social media (Habermas 2023). In any case, there is no denying a connection of sorts between the developing media ecology of the late sixteenth century and the violent urban clashes a half-century later, in London, in Paris, in Barcelona, in Palermo, in Naples, and elsewhere, during the so-called Great Crisis of the seventeenth century, beyond the time frame covered in this Element.

Considering the dynamics of change in Renaissance news, and considering the success of other genres before newspapers, one is almost tempted to think that frequent and regular publishing according to a strict order of emissions might be overrated as a system for getting the news out and feeding the public appetite for such. From the dawn of printing through the first years of the seventeenth century one-off publications regarding one or more related events predominated. What was true of the pre-newspaper Zeitungen in the German-speaking areas was likewise true of the Relaciones de sucesos in Spanish (Baena Sánchez and Espejo Cala 2017: 109). Indeed, long after the advent of handwritten newsletters, the term Avvisi commonly appeared as a title of non-serial news, such as this one printed in Florence in 1572 (USTC No. 1754719): "Avvisi di Vinezia dove s'intende quanto e seguito nella Dalmazia con la presa di Scardona; partita & viaggio per Levante del signor Giovanni d'Austria" [News from Venice where one discovers what happened in Dalmatia with the seizure of Scardona; and the departure and voyage of Don John of Austria]. All these publication types played important roles not only in the printing business, but in people's perceptions of the world.

A rough quantification of these and related productions can be attempted using the tools made available by the USTC, with all possible disclaimers regarding the precision of the result. Necessarily for a resource of such scope, a certain lack of uniformity may be evidenced in data collection from a variety of origins in all the major languages. Keeping this in mind, for the entire period from 1500 through 1599, some 11,730 separate items are listed and described in the category of "News Books," which, applied to the pre-newspaper press appears to indicate works containing news before the advent of strict regularity. Such works account for somewhat more than 3 percent of the total of 347,370 separate items (or editions) listed for those years, according to a survey conducted in April 2025. The number of "News Books" constantly increases throughout the century, with a slight stall in the 1550s, specifically in the year 1552, when news books from the Holy Roman Empire fall to 22 from 45 in the previous year. Due to fear or actual violence in the context of opposition to Emperor Charles V's excessively tolerant religious policies? The connection is difficult to establish.

Also according to the USTC, the geography of "news book" production changes radically across the whole sixteenth century. In the first decade, dozens of cities are named as places of publication, with particular emphasis on Nuremberg, Paris, Strasburg, Augsburg, Venice, and Lyon. By the end of the century, the top places are Germany (no city named), London, Prague, Rome, Nuremberg, Cologne, Paris, and Amsterdam, with Venice somewhat further down the list for this particular category of print. The result is somewhat surprising, considering the Venetian reputation for leadership in the early part of the century. A problem of categorization? An issue regarding the increasingly attentive regulation of this type of publication? We keep in mind that in overall production Venice figures second after Paris in 1500; and by 1590-99 it has returned to the absolute primacy it enjoyed in the late fifteenth century, followed by London and Paris, after which we find Lyon, Rome and Antwerp (Di Filippo Bareggi 1994).

Still, by century's end there was no adequate way to account for events on a regular basis that were already putting stress on the developing industry of printed news. From the dawn of printing, the chatty, sensational, and prediction-filled calendars came out year by year, but they were not periodicals. Periodical news arguably begins with the semi-annual *Messrelationen*, that is, news reports on the previous half-year of occurrences, made available first at the spring and autumn Frankfurt book fairs, and eventually wherever competing fairs occurred. The originator of the practice is said to have been Michael von Aitzing, a multitalented Austrian diplomat and chronicler who eventually settled in Cologne, where he distinguished himself by publishing an account of the recent history of the Low Countries. After emitting a number of accounts of newsworthy items over the duration of a year, in 1588 he conceived of shortening the time between publications and introducing regularity. Thus, in his German-language (but Latin-titled) *Historica Postremae Relationis Appendix* issued in September (USTC No. 663738), he offered "A historical account, of the histories and affairs that occurred since the month of March," as a follow-up to the account he had previously published, with a similar title, in the month of April, setting the pace for regular issues. Matters would be covered, as in the previous booklet, taking place in "the Archbishopric of Cologne, as well as Bonn, and in the Netherlands, France, Germany, Spain, Poland, Denmark, England, and indeed in other places" (Körber 2016).

The mass of material, just for the six-month period, was such that Aitzing could not, or would not, digest it all into a few paragraphs. The result is a 122-page production beginning with a summary making the appropriate inferences from what would be told in the following pages. Next comes a month-by-month account beginning with March, when highlights include the plea of the people of Bonn for the restitution of their city and much else. The section on April includes the Muscovites demanding Maximilian III, Archduke of Austria, as the king of Poland. In May, among other events, diplomats are going back and forth between Spain and England in hopes of negotiating a peace settlement, while the Armada sails out from Lisbon. Also, the Duke of Guise is going to Paris in the midst of the French religious wars. Events continue from month to month: as in June, for instance, when peace between Spain and England fails to materialize, with the Spanish Armada regrouping in Coruña. Also that month Strassburg joins with Bern and Zurich in the Swiss union. July comes and an edict is published in Rouen against the Huguenots. In August there is the conclusion of the Armada story, and boats are arriving in Cascais, near Lisbon, from the Indies. In September we have the arrival of Cardinal Granvelle's brother in Antwerp for peace negotiations. The material over the next six months, and those following, will be treated in separate publications according to this pattern.

Perhaps it was only a matter of time before some eager entrepreneur thought of doing a regular monthly roundup of such matters, and this occurs in 1597 with Samuel Dilbaum, an Augsburg-based educator and writer about current affairs. At the end of January that year he publishes, using a printing house across the Bodensee in the Swiss canton of St. Gallen, a work entitled *"Historische Relatio, oder Erzehlung der fuernembsten Handlungen und Geschichten so sich im Jenner des 1597"* (USTC No. 664901). In the 24 closely printed pages of this booklet, he gave "as briefly as possible, what was worth writing about the month of January from what I had on hand."[27] He begins with

---

[27] www.deutschestextarchiv.de/book/view/anonym_annus_1597?p=1 https://www.deutschestextarchiv.de/book/view/anonym_annus_1597?p=1.

the latest on the Hungarian war, including the visit of the Turkish *chaus* to the residence of the prince of Transylvania in Weißenburg (now Székesfehérvár). Then there is (pp. 13-16) a call by the Prince of Bavaria for troops to fight against the Turks, along with a page-long list of products to be taxed for raising money for arms, as whatever the recruits may already have in their possession are likely inadequate. Next come four pages dedicated to "Italian, Spanish, French and Netherlandish affairs." The last story (p. 24) takes us to Japan, where "The fathers of the Society of Jesus in Iaponia [Japan] have written to their general in Rome although they endured great persecution nonetheless they achieved much benefit. Accordingly, an extremely large number of the same people and pagans including many great personages have taken Christian baptism and come to the faith, and they even have good hope that the same king will become a Christian." Finally the author makes a closing promise that "later I will follow this with what occurred in February." And so he did, repeating the pattern in the following months.

As far as is known, the periodical persisted for one year only, and was provided with a frontispiece for eventual gathering and binding of all fascicles as a single volume called *Annus Christi 1597*. One can imagine that the time involved in putting together a publication of uncertain success may have been a deterrent from other attempts. The care in narrating, and the time devoted to preparing the monthly fascicles of the work, aligned Dilbaum's *Historische Erzehlung* with the many other so-called Zeitungen, the genre of one-off event-specific publications which had been circulating in Germany for many decades. Attention to compositional coherence evinced an awareness even of the historian's art. As was the intention, we are far from the rapid-fire breathlessness of the disconnected accounts in the handwritten newsletters.

For as long as "news books" and semi-periodical news existed, handwritten newsletters, such as those examined in the previous section, continued to epitomize the advantages of speed and immediacy; but the two worlds of printed and manuscript news remained divided, as did the relative audiences, very broad versus mainly elite (Pieper 1992: 190). With the growing reputation and notoriety of the newsletters, not only as sources of crucial information, but also of gossip, entertainment, and even scandal, emphasized from time to time in the numerous official pronouncements purporting to prevent their production and diffusion, the potential for wider distribution began to occur to a few of those involved. Possible dangers in the larger cities, of course, would have been evident to any potential entrepreneur, which likely explains why such places were slow to develop ways to commercialize regular handwritten contents on a wider scale.

We may suppose that the evident risks of genre-relevant experimentation in the news business help explain why the first known attempt to create a weekly printed newspaper occurs in Alsatian Strasbourg, not in one of the chief centers of production. Here, a modest bookseller named Johann Carolus conceived of making the handwritten newsletters the basis for his serial publication, with important features that would serve to protect the practice for years to come (Hillgärtner 2021: chap.1). The absence of a large, well-organized, and legally protected printing industry in the city played in the favor of the somewhat unlikely inventor of the new genre. Already an avid reader and writer of newsletters, he petitioned the city government for a monopoly on his idea in 1605 (Weber 2005). As motives for his request he pointed to the expense of acquiring the necessary newsletters and the small return received from the time-consuming activity of writing up numerous copies by hand for distribution to his subscription list. He had already acquired a printing press. But to gain value from applying the formidable powers of printing to the weekly practice of news production he needed an important guarantee: namely, a local monopoly for his product. At the same time he offered a guarantee of his own: in the sheets there would be nothing but what was circulating already in the newsletters, without any commentary, criticism, or advocacy on his part. The Strasbourg council appears to have conceded.

The weekly paper, entitled *Relation aller Fürnemmen und gedenckwürdigen Historien*, that is, "Account of all important and noteworthy histories," promised to communicate "everything of the most trustworthy sort that I receive." Exactly when printing began is still something of a mystery, as the only extant copies date to 1609 and continue with notable gaps well after the death of Carolus in 1634. Stories in the first available year demonstrated the wide-ranging correspondence of the publisher, in terms of the newsletters he received and probably sent out: from Prague to Antwerp, from Vienna to Venice and Rome, with relative frequencies recorded in Table 4, based on data from Thomas Schröder (1995: 127–130).

Of course, under any of these rubrics there might be stories from yet other places, just as in the handwritten newsletters that formed the basis of his production. For instance, in issue 2 for January 15, in a paragraph headed "From Venice, from the 2nd of the same month" we find a story "from Spain" saying that "the king held a grand procession there to obtain the indulgence of the Jubilee year" and also "ordered the Englishman Anthony Scherlin [Sherley] to equip a grand armada to resist the Dutch ... and that an armada with 3,000 Portuguese sailed from Lisbon to the Portuguese Indies to completely wipe out the Dutch who are said to have allied themselves with the Turks."[28] Again, in issue 6, the report from Cologne dated February 12 asserts that "From England

---

[28] Relation, 1609 n. 2, January 2.

Table 4 Places of origin in the Strasbourg relation, 1609

Place of origin	Number of articles	Number of words
Prague	91	25,471
Vienna	75	16,547
Cologne	51	15,880
Rome	51	10,587
Venice	51	13,869
Antwerp	6	48
Lyon	6	604
The Hague	5	500
Bratislava	5	971
Brussels	4	392
Amsterdam	2	176
Wroclaw	2	1,022
Erfurt	1	185
Frankfurt	1	49
Kaschau	1	112
Cracow	1	257
Linz	1	230
Neustadt	1	300
Novigrad	1	141
Total	358	88,102

it is reported that one of their ships from the East Indies arrived in London timely and in good order," whereas the ships from Holland "were not yet loaded and therefore could not come."[29]

Although no study has yet discovered the particular newsletters from which Carolus drew his material, we may imagine that he proceeded exactly as promised to the Strasbourg authorities. His practice would therefore have been to extract for copy and sale as his own product exactly what was to be found in the regularly circulated handwritten material which he so carefully and expensively collected. The novelty lay not in the contents, but in the method of reproduction, as well as the quantity of material – roughly 570 words per page against 440 words in a typical newsletter, a 30 percent advantage.[30] The success of the operation, at least at first, may be judged to some degree by the absence of any surviving copies of the first four years of operation, if we suppose that the endeavor went ahead as originally planned, immediately following the contact

---

[29] Relation, 1609 n. 6, February 12.   [30] ASF, MdP vol. 3087 fol. 1r, February 12, 1600.

with the Strasburg authorities, and entire press runs were bought up and circulated by eager readers.

Whatever may have been the troubles and triumphs of these first years of the business in Strasbourg, a new pattern had been set, and subsequent mirror attempts rapidly appeared: in Wolfenbüttel in 1609, Frankfurt in 1615, Berlin in 1617, Valencia in 1618, Antwerp in 1620, and so forth (Arblaster 2006, Espejo Cala 2015, Behringer 2017), quickly followed by versions in other lands and languages. The age of the newspaper had begun, and would continue in various guises, until modern times. The new system of communication rapidly became widespread, as did the opinions about the significance. The possible promise for various agendas in the realm of communications now came under discussion; especially considering the potential for reaching wide audiences at relatively low cost. The question soon arose, should governments seize the initiative, in the provision of regular news about the world, couched in acceptable terms?

At first, opinions were mixed. Experience showed that the first step to regular public information would have to be the prohibition of works conveying wrong impressions. In 1621 Paolo Sarpi, consultant to the Venetian government, conveyed his thoughts on the whole question in a report on the effects of a recent political pamphlet. Attributed to Hermann Conrad, baron von Friedenberg, a Habsburg sympathizer in the Thirty Years' War, the work condemned the Venetian government's deal-making with heretical states. Sarpi, well acquainted with the many avenues for diffusion of the written word in the early modern Italian world, had this to say: "They encourage conversation and provide material for the discourses of the disaffected and the self-interested, who insinuate themselves into the open ears of the simple-minded, seducing them and impressing upon them concepts with pernicious effects" (Sarpi 1958: 221). Indeed, during the recent Interdict controversy with the Pope (1606) regarding the relative jurisdictional roles of Church and state, some of the most dangerous fomenters of sedition, armed with the concepts illustrated in enemy pamphlets, had been the preachers.

In the event that written works could not be effectively prohibited, Sarpi supposed, writers might be hired or otherwise encouraged to engage in active literary combat. This too had its perils. First of all, what if the opponent was more humorous than you were? "Never attempt to respond to writings that speak evil with brevity and wit, even if falsely, when the defense requires a long narrative or discourse, since brief and witty expressions impress themselves on and take over the mind, whereas a long discourse tires it to such an extent that it will never open up to the truth"

(Sarpi 1958: 222). Next, what if the defense could be more damaging than the criticism itself? Even the truth can sometimes hurt, Sarpi noted. For the public dealings of a government, based on a calculus of the lesser evil, were bound to appear suspect to an ignorant private person bound to conventional morality – who might for instance recoil at the thought of Catholics making deals with heretics.

> No state has been nor can be without very great imperfections .... The [Venetian] Republic is by no means immune to the human condition. Its defects could be exposed and censured and used to condemn the whole government by anyone who wants to offend and create a bad impression; they cannot be defended, can scarcely be hidden, and to make excuse for them is to admit them, even though human malice does not listen to excuses anyway.

Faced with the futility of all the other alternatives to controlling information, Sarpi made a startling break with the past. The best strategy, he suggested, was to combat information with more information. One could pay attention to events as they occurred and publish a narration of them with arguments supporting the side that fits one's interests and increases one's advantage. By offering readers their first taste of what was going on in the world and tinting information in the proper way, the government could ensure that information from other sources would be discounted or ignored. However, having come so far, Sarpi drew back. He rejected his own suggestion as soon as he made it; and his reasons reveal still more about ideas concerning information in the new emerging world of the printed newspapers. The gesture of verbal defense and explanation of policies placed the government in an attitude of subservience to the audience and opened up the secrets of state unnecessarily to private persons. This was to be avoided at all costs. Said Sarpi:

> Everyone confesses that the true way of ruling the subject is to keep him ignorant of and reverent toward public affairs, since when he finds out about them he gradually begins to judge the prince's actions; he becomes so accustomed to this communication that he believes it is due him and when it is not given, he sees a false significance or else perceives an affront and conceives hatred – and what is said of subjects can be applied mutatis mutandis to neighbors. This reason is so strong that it has no response in cases where [the arguments of the government] have not [yet] been published and where its opponents are not expected to publish contrary ones; in such cases the subject would not be kept in ignorance and reverence, but the door would be opened to the contrary opinion formed by the reading of opposing manifestoes, which the public service insists must be prohibited and once diffused must be eradicated. (Sarpi 1958: 230)

Making the subject think about politics could open a Pandora's box. So, having rejected his own best suggestion, Sarpi gave up.

Around the same time in England, a group of petitioners including John Pory and Thomas Locke apparently lacked such scruples, or ignored them. Both had experience in the world of manuscript newsletters; and in their view, the best way to shake people out of their natural torpor and bring them under the right rule of reason was by regularly "spreading among them such reports as may best make for that matter to which we would have them drawn" (cited in Mousley 1991: 159). This might accordingly "disperse into the veynes of the whole body of a state such matter as may best temper it, & be most agreeable to the disposition of the head & the principale members," in other words, drawing them toward the decisions of king, Church and Parliament, "upon all occasions that shall be offered." The interesting idea for official news publication was apparently entertained for a time; but as print culture moved forever forward, the various efforts to bring the idea to fruition, by Nathaniel Butter and others, were overtaken by events – commercial as well as political.

The closest approximation of an official newspaper in this period therefore turned out to be the French *Gazette*, begun in 1631 by the scholar-publisher Theophraste Renaudot, and closely monitored by Cardinal Richelieu, the state secretary of French King Louis XIII, with appropriate references to "our forces" and the "enemy armies" and so forth, as well as favorable accounts of ceremonials taking place in France to celebrate the monarchy (Feyel: 2000: ch. 3–4). Granted a monopoly on the provision of regular printed news, the paper (Figure 5) had no rivals in all of France, although reprints were allowed in the provinces to guarantee a wider circulation (Feyel 1982). The conditions were ripe for still further fundamental changes, but by this time, we are outside our period, so our story ends here.

Then as now, misinformation worked best in darkness – when unobstructed by education, discussion, dissent, and the human desire for knowledge. Eventually literacy would begin to rise, contraband information would keep crossing borders, and people, at least sometimes, were able to keep an open mind. Indeed, the technology of the time, just as the relevant state institutions, in spite of all aspirations, afforded no practical means, possessed no approximation of the efficiency that would later become possible in later societies. The systematic molding of the mind regarding current events, carried out as a calculated affront to human dignity, was still many centuries away; and likewise distant was the notion of freedom of thought as a human right. Renaissance news was only the beginning, not the end.

GAZETTE

E Roy de Perse auec 15. mille cheuaux & 50. mille hommes de pied affiege Dille à deux iournées de la ville de Babylone : où le grand Seigneur a fait faire commandement à tous ses Ianissaires de se rendre sous peine de la vie, & continuë nonobstant ce divertissement-là à faire tousiours vne aspre guerre aux preneurs de Tabac, qu'il fait suffoquer à la fumée. *De Constantinople le 2. Avril 1632.*

Sa Saincteté a finalement receu les articles & conditions accordées concernant la paix si long temps atttenduë en Italie. Il est survenu dans Madril vn accident de feu qui a fort endommagé l'hostel du Comte Olivarez, & le Palais Royal. Sa Majesté Catholique a pourveu le Marquis d'Ayton de la charge de General de la marine en la coste de Flandres, & a envoyé Dom Ferdinand Contieras pour haster le partement de la flotte de Vestinde. Le Clergé contribuë en Portugal deux cens vingt-cinq mil escus pour subvenir à la necessité presente des affaires. *De Rome le 26. Avril*

La ville d'Vlm a refusé ouvertement la contribution que le Commissaire Imperial luy demandoit, & respondu au Magistrat qu'ils acceptoyent la resolution de l'assemblee de Lipsic. On fait marcher contr'eux les Regimes d'Italie : Mais on croit que le passage leur sera refusé par ceux de Sueve & Franconie, qui ont desia leué force Soldats. *De la haute Allemagne le 30. Avril.*

Les Imperialistes se sont icy arrestez apres la prise de Francfort sur Oder, & attendent mille Hongrois que le Palatin leur doit enuoyer, qui se ioindront à la garnison de Landsberg, & autres trouppes dot Tilly les doit grossir, capables de resister desormais aux Suedois entrez en la Sylesie. *De Freistad en Sylesie le 1. May.*

Les Espagnols ne sont point contents, & ne trouvent point seur pour l'Estat de Milan que les passages de Savoye soyent gardez par les Suisses, & dit-on que *los Grandes* promettent d'entretenir 40000. hommes si l'on continuë la guerre. A quoy les François repliquent, sans se haster, qu'ils ne rendront point ce qu'ils tiennent sans vne bonne execution du traitté de la part des autres. *De Venise le 2. May*

On leve des gens de guerre par toute l'Autriche, Sylesie, Moravie, Boheme, Bavieres, & païs circonvoisins, qui donneront bien des affaires au Roy de Suede. Le Burgraue de Dona est retourné en Sylesie y prendre la conduitte des armees. On ne doute plus de la paix d'Italie, ny de celle de Transsilvanie. On a iey publié vn Edict portant que chaque maison payera deux florins dans le premier de May prochain. Le fils de l'Empereur assisté du Duc de Fridland, s'en va en qualité de Generalissime conduire les trouppes qui retournent d'Italie, ausquelles se doivent ioindre 24. mille hommes que ledit Duc de Fridland *De Vienne le 3. May.*

A

Figure 5 Page from an issue of the French *Gazette* from the year 1632 (Gallica)

Conclusion

When Antonio Morosini began an early fifteenth-century diary entry with "we have news" regarding events occurring in more or less distant locations from which communications were expected, he could hardly have imagined the precious traces he might be leaving. A worldwide network was in the making, whose various ramifications and general contours, amid many discontinuities, would reach across time and space even to the twenty-first century. He only wished to transmit, to his own family and those of the other patricians involved in running the Venetian Republic, an account of important occurrences such as the recent struggle against Milan, including hints about where the news came from (Christ 2005). But the system of information exchange, built at the dawn of the Renaissance and experienced by Morosini and his contemporaries, was to have far reaching consequences.

In time, more and more people would carry on their lives, goods would move, battles would join, cities would celebrate, in coordination with what was heard or inferred from circuits of information that delivered, first sporadically then weekly or biweekly, and eventually more often, reports on the changing economic, social, political realities of the day. In this Element we have tried to show how a few barely perceptible characteristics of a news-driven society began to emerge some time between the fourteenth and fifteenth centuries in Europe, with some aspects reaching maturity in the sixteenth century and later. Seventeenth-century events such as the Thirty Years War, the Civil Wars in England and the 1640s civil disturbances elsewhere proved to be particularly powerful forces for increasing curiosity and interest, ushering in a period of ever-sharper questioning of reigning orthodoxies, with which we close the volume. But the connection between past and present is far more fraught than any summary can convey here.

Rather than a decisive march from the oral to the written, from writing to printing, we observe an early modern world in which handwritten newsletters persisted in many places until the early eighteenth century and were by no means displaced by new technology (Degl'Innocenti, Richardson and Sbordoni, eds. 2016, Palmieri 2018, Ezell 2019). The media ecology of the period featured multiple means of production, each drawing upon the other – oral, handwritten, printed. The lively interaction between visual and discursive means of expression provided a constant reminder that there was more than one way to convey the exciting, the dreadful, and even the purely routine events of the time, depending on target audience, geographical location, and much else. Indeed, further investigation of these features is currently one of the most promising trends in the study of early news.

Future work on Renaissance news will include not only the multiple media, but the multiple points of departure and arrival of particular stories, viewed as a space of flows throughout much of Europe and the Mediterranean and beyond, with careful attention to the news-bearing words themselves, acting as vehicles for ideas about the world, the society, the self, and everything in between – at times knitting people together across vast distances, at times driving them apart. In a wide-ranging synthesis of the whole period and beyond, summarizing current scholarship and making abundant use of recently digitized sources, Joad Raymond, in his recent contribution (2025), directs attention to "collective and combined acts of communication, the stories people shared, how they did so, the way this bound them together, the world they made," adding that "it is a fundamentally human story, but one that unfolds on an impersonal scale."

In terms of the industrial components of news in the age of the hand press, these would change gradually along with printing per se, picking up considerable speed and incisiveness only after the turn of the nineteenth century. Before the advent of the steam press, hand presses themselves could only become sturdier and more smoothly operable. Meanwhile, copper-plate engraving eventually submerged traditional woodcut illustrations. Paper making became more widely diffused, especially in places with abundant clear water for the still rag-based operation. On the human side, firms became larger with more personnel and some gained significant international connections: the Plantin in Antwerp, Elzevier in Leyden. Meanwhile, the politics of information became a serious concern of every state, and increasingly, of the people therein.

Sixteenth-century critics of knowledge at the time were well aware of the many pitfalls and threats. Taking for granted the evident absurdity of relying, for a picture of the world, entirely on information from news publications, theorists discussing the next levels of intellectual elaboration – for instance, historiography – decried the mistakes, manipulations, and evident falsehoods. Even though historians still mostly preferred to leave the remote past to the pioneers of historiography in ancient Greece and Rome, the reliance, for later events, on recent or contemporary testimonies, as well as upon one's own interpretative inclination, could lead, many thought, to serious mistakes.

Francesco Patrizi, a Neoplatonic philosopher and professor at the University of Padua, in a dialogue "On the Truth of History" published in 1560, was one of many suggesting that bad historians and erroneous histories were due, among other things, to unreliable sources (Patrizi 1560: 29 r, Vasoli 1989). Unreliable sources, in turn, existed because the people most likely to have the most accurate insider information about events were ministers privy to a prince's secret counsels. Yet precisely these ministers were the most likely to convey such counsels in a modified form. Given the pressure of reputation on the prince as well as the minister, manipulation of the truth was almost inevitable. And even when there was no obvious manipulation, the documentary or oral accounts of a particular event were subject to an endless process of substitutions and omissions caused by the defective or selective memory of those involved. The most trustworthy accounts probably came from eyewitnesses who took a neutral stance toward the events. But those who took such a stance usually did so because they simply did not understand what they saw. Therefore, they likely overlooked important details that helped explain interests and actions. Moreover, general narratives were more likely to be truthful than specific ones. But the more general an account, the less useful it was likely to be. And when historians, lacking the necessary evidence for specific episodes, attempted to add details and causal hypotheses to their overly general accounts, they risked sacrificing truth in favor of didacticism. Similar criticisms could be made of news accounts.

The epistemological head cold of the sixteenth century, in regard to the search for truth about events, became the pneumonia of the following century (Dooley 1999: ch. 4, Burke 2000: ch. 9). Pierre Bayle, the Rotterdam-based polymath, in his *Historical and critical dictionary*, made skepticism about a system of political communication dominated by passions and interests part of a much broader questioning of the usual sources of knowledge. He focused his attention on the wars of words between Catholics and Protestants in the late seventeenth century and wondered whether the truth about any event described by one side or the other could ever truly be known. And if the errors of historical works were compounded by the reliance on reports and documents disseminated by newspaper writers seeking quick profit through sensationalism and flattery, the unreliability of the results was enough to drive the serious reader to distraction. "There is no greater damage," he remarked, "than that which can be done to historical monuments" (Bayle [1709] 1740: IV, Appendix, 10). As a result, he suspected, many of his contemporaries had ceased to believe in history altogether. "And their conclusion begins with the newspapers and extends to the entire spectrum of civil historians who compile their rhapsodies from only these miserable sources." The only mistake of true skeptics, he argued, was to consider the lack of evidence for the existence of worldly things as a reason for atheism, rather than an invitation to fideism. The truths of faith, like the truths of the world, are probably not rationally intelligible at all, he argued. Other thinkers would attempt a restructuring of knowledge and methods of discovery to place things on a more solid footing. But at this point the cultural stream begins to flow into the more general currents of the European pre-Enlightenment; and we are already far beyond the scope of this Element.

More recently, the widespread use of mechanically diffused propaganda gave rise to manuals by Edward Bernays and communications theories by Leonard Doob and Harold Lasswell. And regimes that have thrived on the inculcation, by constant repetition and denial, of a particular view of contemporary events plainly contrary to proven facts, continue to surface from time to time, even in the more stable democracies. "Doublethink" and its communications corollary "Newspeak" was supposed by George Orwell, in his 1949 novel, to have belonged to a future dystopian society that existed in 1984. Signs of the work's enduring appeal have been particularly abundant in recent years, indicating a widespread awareness of the risks ahead.

As far as the simple and dispassionate communication of events is concerned, some modern studies express doubts arising from the inherent contradictions. Winfried Schulz, in a work entitled "The construction of reality in the news media," points out that any account is likely to be partial or selective in some way. Indeed, the more a report corresponds to what journalists consider to be the important and therefore newsworthy aspects of reality, the greater its newsworthiness will be. What is not newsworthy does not get reported, although the particular features that are to be ignored or favored may change with the changing tastes. Given this structure of news transmission, there is no way of precisely measuring to what extent the media distort or falsify the flow of news. All things considered, "What really happened, and what is the correct picture of reality, is ultimately a metaphysical question" (Schulz 1976). What then is the curious citizen supposed to do?

Taking as inevitable that political regimes and their societies will have their own convenient ways of remembering things, William H. McNeill (1982) once referred to historiography as "the care and repair of public myth." The task of the diligent investigator, he suggested, is to set the record straight to any possible extent, for the benefit of those willing to listen. More recently, Adriano Prosperi (2025) has drawn attention to the impossibility of changing or erasing the past per se, understood as something that actually occurred, in spite of all attempts to cancel whatever does not suit current tastes. An abiding conviction regarding the accuracy of this formulation is still shared within various professional categories including journalists and historians. Here we end on a hopeful note regarding the news media, that constant care for the sources and the meanings, and rigorous education concerning the history and the methods of analysis, may induce a more critical perspective among makers as well as users.

References

Primary Sources

Alberti, L. B. (1972). *On Painting and On Sculpture: The Latin Texts of De Pictura and De Statua*. Edited and translated by C. Grayson. London: Phaidon Press.

Aquinas, T. (1975). *Summa Contra Gentiles*. Bk. 3: *Providence, Part 2*. Edited and translated by V. J. Bourke. Notre Dame: University of Notre Dame.

Archivio di Stato di Firenze (1990). *Carteggio universale di Cosimo I de' Medici: Inventario*, vol. 9: 1556–1559, ed. M. Morviducci. Milan: Giunta regionale toscana & Editrice Bibliografica.

Aristotle (1984). *Poetics*. Translated by I. Bywater. In *The Rhetoric and Poetics of Aristotle*. Introduction by E. P. J. Corbett. New York: McGraw-Hill.

Baronius, C. ([1588–1607] 1880) *Annales Ecclesiastici*, vol. 29. Brussels: Guerin.

Bayle, P. ([1709] 1740). *Dictionnaire historique et critique*. Amsterdam: P. Brunel.

Boccaccio, G. (1981). *Decameron*. Ed. M. Marti and E. Ceva Valla. Milan: Rizzoli.

Bruni, L. (2001). *History of the Florentine People*: Books 1–4. Edited and translated by J. Hankins. Cambridge, MA: Harvard University Press.

Bruni, L. (2007). *History of the Florentine People*: Books 9–12. Edited and translated by J. Hankins with D. J. W. Bradley. Cambridge, MA: Harvard University Press.

Bullarum. (1826–84). *Bullarum diplomatum et privilegiorum sanctorum romanorum pontificum Taurinensis editio*. Naples: Caporaso.

Chaucer, G. (2008). *The Riverside Chaucer*. Ed. L. D. Benson. Oxford: Oxford University Press.

Codogno, O. (1608). *Nuovo Itinerario delle Poste*. Milan: Bordoni.

Cotrugli, B. ([1573] 2016). *Libro de l'arte de la mercatura*, ed. V. Ribaudo, preface by T. Zanato. Venice: Edizioni à Foscari

Erasmus, D. (1906). *Opus Epistolarum Erasmi*. Edited by P. S. Allen. Oxford, Clarendon Press.

Erasmus, D. (1997). *Colloquies*, tr. C. R. Thompson. Toronto: University of Toronto Press.

Franco, V. (1580). *Lettere familiari a diversi*. Venice: n.p.

Gairdner, J. (1904). *The Paston Letters, A.D. 1422–1509*. New Complete Library Edition. London: Chatto and Windus.

Guillaume d'Auvergne (1591). *Opera omnia*. Venice: Zenaro.

Klarwill, V. von (1924). *The Fugger News-Letters, Being a Selection of unpublished letters from the Correspondents of the House of Fugger during the years 1568–1605*. Translation by P. de Chary. London: John Lane.

Lancellotti, L. (1636). *L' Hoggidi: Overo Gl'Ingegni Non Inferiori à' passati*. Venice: Guerigli.

Machiavelli, N. ([1522] 2007). "Memoriale a Raffaello Girolami quando ai 23 d'ottobre partì per Spagna all'Imperatore." In *Opere*, vol. 43: *Istorie fiorentine e altre opere storiche e politiche*, ed. A. Montevecchi. Turin: UTET, 226–227.

Matraini, C. ([1595] 2018). *Lettere e Rime*. Introduction and commentary by C. Acucella. Florence: Florence University Press.

More, T. (1516/1967). *Utopia*. Translated by J. P. Dolan. In J. J. Greene and J. P. Dolan, eds., The Essential Thomas More. New York: New American Library.

Patrizi, F. (1560). *Della Historia dieci dialoghi*. Venice: Andrea Arrivabene.

Prothero, G. W. (1898). *Select Statutes and Other Constitutional Documents Illustrative of the Reigns of Elizabeth and James I*. Oxford: Clarendon Press.

Sansovino, F. (1584). *Del Secretario*, Venice: Cornelio Arrivabene.

Sanuto [Sanudo], M. (1879–1904). *I Diarii*, F. Stefani, N. Barozzi, G. Berchet, M. Allegri eds. 58 vols. Venice: Visentini.

Sarpi, Paolo (1958). *Scritti giurisdizionalistici*, ed. G. Gambarin. Bari: Laterza.

Tasso, T. (1582). *Il Messaggero*, dialogo. Venice: Giunti.

Villani, G. (1991). *Nuova Cronica*. Edited by G. Porta. 3 vols. Fondazione Pietro Bembo. Parma: Ugo Guanda Editore.

Watt, D. (2004). *The Paston Women: Selected Letters*. Martlesham, Suffolk: Boydell and Brewer.

Secondary Sources

Acidini Luchinat, C. (1993). *Benozzo Gozzoli, la Cappella dei Magi*. Milan: Electa.

Allen, E. J. B. (1972). *Post and Courier Service in the Diplomacy of Early Modern Europe*. The Hague: Martinus Nijhoff.

Arblaster, P. (2006). "Posts, Newsletters, Newspapers: England in a European System of Communications." In J. Raymond, ed., *News Networks in Seventeenth Century Britain and Europe*. London: Routledge, pp. 19–34.

Arblaster, P., Belo, A., Espejo Cala, C., et al. (2016). "The Lexicons of Early Modern News." In Raymond, J. and N. Moxham, eds. *News Networks in Early Modern Europe*. Leyden: Brill, pp. 64-101.

Baars, R. (2021). *Rumours of Revolt: Civil War and the Emergence of a Transnational News Culture in France and the Netherlands, 1561–1598*. Leyden: Brill.

Baena Sánchez, F. and Espejo Cala, C. (2017). "En busca de un vocabulario compartido para describir y representar el periodismo de la Edad Moderna." In G. Ciappelli and V. Nider, eds. *La invención de las noticias: Las relaciones de sucesos entre la literatura y la información (siglos XVI-XVIII)*. Trento: Università degli Studi di Trento.

Barbarics-Hermanik, Z. (2010). "Handwritten Newsletters as Interregional Information Sources in Central- and Southeastern Europe." In B. Dooley, ed. *The Dissemination of News and the Emergence of Contemporaneity in Early Modern Europe*. London: Ashgate, 155–178.

Barbarics-Hermanik, Z. (2012). "The Coexistence of Manuscript and Print: Handwritten Newsletters in the Second Century of Print, 1540–1640." In M. Walsby and G. Kemp, eds. *The Book Triumphant: Print in Transition in the Sixteenth and Seventeenth Centuries*. Leiden: Brill, 347–368

Barker, S. (2016). "'Secret and Uncertain': A History of Avvisi at the Court of the Medici Grand Dukes." In J. Raymond, and N. Moxham, eds. *News Networks in Early Modern Europe*. Leyden: Brill, 716–738.

Baron, S. A. (2001). "The Guises of Dissemination in Early Seventeenth-Century England: News in Manuscript and Print." In S. A. Baron and B. Dooley, eds., *The Politics of Information in Early Modern Europe*. London: Routledge, 41–56.

Baron, S. A. (2010). "Pory, John (1572–1633) of London." In A. Thrush and J. P. Ferris, eds. *The History of Parliament: the House of Commons 1604–1629*. Cambridge: Cambridge University Press, https://www.historyofparliamentonline.org/volume/1604-1629/member/pory-john-1572-1633.

Bauer, O. (2011). *Zeitungen vor der Zeitung. Die Fuggerzeitungen (1568–1605) und das frühmoderne Nachrichtensystem*. (Colloquia Augustana, vol. 28.) Berlin: Akademie.

Bechtel, G. (1992). *Gutenberg et l'invention de l'imprimerie: Une enquête*. Paris: Fayard.

Behringer, W. (2003). *Im Zeichen des Merkur—Reichspost und Kommunikationsrevolution in der frühen Neuzeit*. Göttingen: Vandenhoeck & Ruprecht.

Behringer, W. (2006). "Communications Revolutions: A Historiographical Concept." *German History*, 24, No. 3: 333–74.

Behringer, W. (2017). "The Invention of a News Medium: The First Printed Periodical Newspapers in Strasbourg (1605), Wolfenbüttel (1609) and Frankfurt (1615)." In G. Ciappelli and V. Nider, eds. *La invención de las noticias: Las relaciones de sucesos entre la literatura y la información (siglos XVI–XVIII)*. Trent: Università degli Studi di Trento, 54–76.

Benedict, P. (2007). *Graphic History: The "Wars, Massacres and Troubles" of Tortorel and Perrissin*. Geneva: Droz.

Biow, D. (2002). *Doctors, Ambassadors, Secretaries: Humanism and Profession in Renaissance Italy*. Chicago: Chicago University Press.

Botelho, K. (2009). *Renaissance Earwitness: Rumor and Early Modern Masculinity*. New York: Palgrave Macmillan.

Brandi, C. ed. (1983). *Palazzo pubblico di Siena: Vicende costruttive e decorazione*. Milan: Silvana Editoriale.

Braudel, F. (1972). *The Mediterranean and the Mediterranean World in the Age of Philip II*. Translated by Sian Reynolds. 2 vols. London: Collins.

Briggs, A., and Burke, P. (2009). *A Social History of the Media: From Gutenberg to the Internet*. Cambridge, MA: Polity.

Burgio, E. (2024). "Le Asie di Marco Polo (descrivere le 'diversità del mondo')." In E. Burgio and S. Simion, eds., *Marco Polo. Storia e mito di un viaggio e di un libro*. Rome: Carocci, vol. 1, 309–338.

Buringh, E. and Van Zanden, J. L. (2009). "Charting the 'Rise of the West': Manuscripts and Printed Books in Europe, a Long-Term Perspective from the Sixth through Eighteenth Centuries." *The Journal of Economic History*, 69, No. 2: 409–445.

Burke, P. (1999). "Erasmus and the Republic of Letters." *European Review*, 7, No. 1: 5–17.

Burke, P. (2000). *A Social History of Knowledge: From Gutenberg to Diderot*. Cambridge: Polity Press.

Burns, K. (2005). "Notaries, Truth, and Consequences." *American Historical Review*, 110: 350–379.

Caizzi, B. (1993). *Dalla posta dei re alla posta di tutti: Territorio e communicazioni in Italia dal XVI secolo all'unità*. Milan: Franco Angeli.

Caplan, J. (2016). *Postal Culture in Europe: 1500–1800*. Oxford: Voltaire Foundation.

Capp, B. (2003). *When Gossips Meet: Women, Family and Neighbourhood in Early Modern England*. Oxford: Oxford University Press.

Certeau, M. de (1984). *The Practice of Everyday Life*, tr. S. Randall. Berkeley: University of California Press.

Christ, G. (2005). "A Newsletter in 1419? Antonio Morosini's Chronicle in the Light of Commercial Correspondence between Venice and Alexandria. *Mediterranean Historical Review*, 20, No. 1: 35–66.

Clemens, R. (2008). "Medieval Maps in a Renaissance Context: Gregorio Dati." In Richard J. A. Talbert and R. W. Unger, eds. *Cartography in Antiquity and the Middle Ages: Fresh Perspectives, New Methods*. Leiden: Brill, 237–256.

Cochrane, E. (1981). *Historians and Historiography in the Italian Renaissance*. Chicago: University of Chicago Press.

Contini, A. and Volpini, P. (2007). *Istruzioni agli ambasciatori e inviati medicei in Spagna e nell' 'Italia spagnola'(1536–1648)*, vol. 1: *1536–1586*. Rome: Ministero per i beni e le attività culturali.

Cressy, D. (1980). *Literacy and the Social Order: Reading and Writing in Tudor and Stuart England*. Cambridge: Cambridge University Press.

Cressy, D. (1989). *Bonfires and Bells: National Memory and the Protestant Calendar in Elizabethan and Stuart England*. Berkeley: University of California Press.

Crinò, A. M. (1969). "Avvisi di Londra di Petruccio Ubaldini, fiorentino, relativi agli anni 1579–1594, con notizie sulla guerra di Fiandra." *Archivio Storico Italiano*, 127, 4, No. 464: 461–581.

De Vivo, F. (2007). *Information and Communication in Venice: Rethinking Early Modern Politics*. Oxford: Oxford University Press.

Degl'Innocenti, L., B. Richardson and C. Sbordoni, eds. (2016). *Interactions Between Orality and Writing in Early Modern Italian Culture*. London and New York: Routledge.

Delumeau, J. (1957–9). *La vie économique et sociale de Rome dans la seconde moitié du XVIe siècle*, 2 vols., Bibliothèque des Écoles Françaises d'Athène et de Rome, 184. Paris: École française de Rome.

Di Filippo Bareggi, C. (1994). "L'editoria Veneziana fra '500 e '600." In G. Cozzi and P. Prodi, eds. *Storia di Venezia*, vol. 6: *Dal Rinascimento al Barocco*. Roma: Istituto della Enciclopedia italiana, 615–648.

Dickens, A. G. (1968). *Reformation and Society in Sixteenth-Century Europe*. New York: Harcourt, Brace and World.

Dohrn-van Rossum, G. (1996). *History of the Hour: Clocks and Modern Temporal Orders*. Translated by T. Dunlap. Chicago: University of Chicago Press.

Dooley, B. (1999). *The Social History of Skepticism: Experience and Doubt in Early Modern Culture*. Baltimore: Johns Hopkins University Press.

Dooley, B. (2005). "Sources and Methods in Information History: the Case of Medici Florence, the Armada and the Siege of Ostend." In J. Koopmans, ed.,

News and Politics in Early Modern Europe, 1500–1800. Leuven: Peeters, 29–46.

Dooley, B. (2014). *A Mattress Maker's Daughter: the Renaissance Romance of Don Giovanni de' Medici and Livia Vernazza.* Cambridge, MA: Harvard University Press.

Dooley, B. (2026). "Brotherly Love: Ferdinando and Don Giovanni Between Rivalry and Affection." In Carla D'Arista and O. Schiavone, eds. *A Companion to Ferdinando I*, Leiden: Brill.

Dover, P. M. (2021). *The Information Revolution in Early Modern Europe: New Approaches to European History.* Cambridge: Cambridge University Press.

Droste, H. (2018). *Das Geschäft mit Nachrichten: Ein barocker Markt für soziale Ressourcen.* Bremen: Edition Lumière.

Dubbini, R. (2002). *Geography of the Gaze: Urban and Rural Vision in Early Modern Europe.* Translated by L. G. Cochrane. Chicago: University of Chicago Press.

Eire, C. M. N. (1989). *War Against the Idols: The Reformation of Worship from Erasmus to Calvin.* Cambridge: Cambridge University Press.

Eisenstein, E. (1979). *The Printing Press as an Agent of Change: Communications and Cultural Transformations in Early-Modern Europe.* Cambridge: Cambridge University Press.

Espejo Cala, C, and Baena, F. (2015). "A Critique of Periodicity in Early Modern Journalism. The First Spanish Serial Gazette: Gazeta de Roma in Valencia (1618–1620)." *European Review*, 23, No. 3: 341–353.

Ettinghausen, H. (2016) "International Relations: Spanish, Italian, French, English and German Printed Single Event Newsletters Prior to Renaudot's Gazette." In J. Raymond, and N. Moxham, eds. *News Networks in Early Modern Europe.* Leiden: Brill, 261–79.

Ezell, M. J. M. (2019). "Manuscript and Print Cultures 1500–1700." In I. Berensmeyer, G. Buelens and M. Demoor, eds. *The Cambridge Handbook of Literary Authorship.* Cambridge: Cambridge University Press, 115–132.

Farge, G. K. (1989). "Early Censorship in Paris: A New Look at the Roles of the Parlement of Paris and of King Francis I." *Renaissance and Reformation / Renaissance et Réforme, New Series / Nouvelle Série*, 13, No. 2: 173–183.

Febvre, L. (1966). *Studi su Riforma e Rinascimento e altri scritti su problemi di metodo e di geografia storica.* Translated by C. Vivanti, preface by D. Cantimori. Turin: Einaudi.

Feyel, G. (1982). *La "Gazette" en province à travers ses réimpressions, 1631–1752.* Amsterdam and Maarssen: APA-Holland University Press.

Feyel, G. (2000). *L'annonce et la nouvelle : La presse d'information en France sous l'Ancien Régime, 1630–1788.* Oxford: Voltaire Foundation.

Fox, A. (2002). *Oral and Literate Culture in England 1500–1700*. Oxford: Oxford University Press.

Fragnito, G. (1992). "Gli ordini religiosi tra Riforma e Controriforma." In M. Rosa, ed., *Clero e società nell'Italia moderna*. Rome and Bari: Laterza, 115–205.

Gallagher J. (2024). "Migrant Voices in Multilingual London, 1560–1600." *Transactions of the Royal Historical Society*, 2: 39–61.

Geertz, C. (1993). "Centers, Kings and Charisma." In C. Geertz, ed., *Local Knowledge: Further Essays in Interpretive Anthropology*. London: Fontana, 121–146.

Geisberg, M., and Strauss, W. L. (1974). *The German Single-Leaf Woodcut, 1500–1550*. New York: Hacker Art Books.

Giansante, M. (1975). "Cappello, Annibale." *Dizionario Biografico degli Italiani*, 18, https://www.treccani.it/enciclopedia/annibale-cappello_(Dizionario-Biografico)/.

Goody, J. (1977). *The Domestication of the Savage Mind*. Cambridge: Cambridge University Press.

Habermas, J. (2023). *A New Structural Transformation of the Public Sphere and Deliberative Politics*. Tr. Ciaran Cronin. Cambridge, MA: Polity.

Harline, C. (1987). *Pamphlets, Printing and Political Culture in the Early Dutch Republic*. Boston: Martinus Nijhoff.

Harvey, D. (1990). "Between Space and Time: Reflections on the Geographical Imagination." *Annals of the Association of American Geographers*, 80: 418–434.

Henneton, L. and L. H. Roper, eds. (2016). *Fear and the Shaping of Early American Societies*. Leiden: Brill.

Herzfeld, M. (1972). "New Light on the 1480 Siege of Rhodes." *The British Museum Quarterly*, 36, No. 3–4: 69–73.

Hillgärtner, J. (2021). *News in Times of Conflict: The Development of the German Newspaper, 1605–1650*. Leiden: Brill.

Houston, R. A. (2002). *Literacy in Early Modern Europe*. London: Routledge.

Infelise, M. (2002). *Prima dei giornali: Alle origini della pubblica informazione*. Milan: Feltrinelli.

Infelise, M. (2018). *Gazzetta: Storia di una parola*. Venice: Marsilio.

Keller, K. and Molino, P. (2015). *Die Fuggerzeitungen im Kontext. Zeitungssammlungen im Alten Reich und in Italien* (Mitteilungen des Instituts für Österreichische Geschichtsforschung, vol. 59) Vienna: Böhlau.

Kittler, J. (2020). "'The Pen is so Noble and Excellent an Instrument': How the Medieval Merchants and Renaissance Diplomats Invented the Newswriting Style." *Journalism Studies*, 21, No. 10: 1403–1419.

Körber, E.-B. (2016). *Messrelationen. Geschichte der deutsch- und lateinischsprachigen "messentlichen" Periodika von 1588 bis 1805*. Bremen: Edition Lumière.

Kreuze, W. (2023). *Things in Time. A Synchronic Analysis of Manuscript Newsletters*. PhD thesis, University College Cork.

Kudella, C. (2016). *The Correspondence Network of Erasmus of Rotterdam. A Data-driven Exploration*. PhD thesis, University College Cork.

Lamal, N. (2023). *Italian Communication on the Revolt in the Low Countries (1566–1648)*. Leiden and Boston: Brill.

Landes, D. (2000[2]). *Revolution in Time: Clocks and the Making of the Modern World*. Cambridge, MA: Harvard University Press.

Le Roy Ladurie, E. (1974). "L'histoire Immobile." *Annales. Histoire, Sciences Sociales*, 29, No. 3: 673–692.

Mack, P. (2011). *A History of Renaissance Rhetoric, 1380–1620*. Oxford: Oxford University Press.

Mansutti S., Kreuze, W., Paltrinieri, C. et al. (2024). "1600: A Year to Remember." In B. Dooley and S. Wilkinson, eds. *Exciting News! Event, Narration and Impact from Past to Present*. Leiden: Brill, 15–40.

Mansutti, S. (2024). *News from Venice: A Digital Analysis of Cosimo Bartoli's Correspondence and Newsletters (1562–1572)*. PhD thesis, University College Cork.

Martens, P. (2024). "Hieronymus Cock's Battle Prints Reconsidered in Light of his Siege of Centallo." *Print Quarterly*, 41, No. 2: 123–140.

Martin, H.-J. (1988). *The History and Power of Writing*. Translated by L. Cochrane. University of Chicago Press.

Mattingly, G. (1959). *The Defeat of the Spanish Armada*. London: Jonathan Cape.

McNeill, W. H. (1982). "The Care and Repair of Public Myth." *Foreign Affairs*, 61, No. 1: 1–13.

Melis, F. (1972). *Documenti per la storia economica dei secoli XIII-XVI*. Florence: Olschki.

Molino, P. (2015). "*Sibenbürgischen corriers mündtlich anzaigen*—Per lettere di Transilvania: Die Fuggerzeitungen im Kontext italienischer Sammlungen." In K. Keller and P. Molino, eds., *Die Fuggerzeitungen im Kontext. Zeitungssammlungen im Alten Reich und in Italien* (Mitteilungen des Instituts für Österreichische Geschichtsforschung, vol. 59) Vienna: Böhlau. 137–83.

Monti, G. G. (2019). "La trattatistica umanistico-rinascimentale italiana sul segretario. Il contributo di Francesco Sansovino." *Politics: Rivista di Studi Politici*, 12, No. 2: 1–20.

Mousley, A. (1991). "Self, State and Seventeenth-Century News." *The Seventeenth Century*, 6: 149–68.

Nussdorfer, L. (2009). *Brokers of Public Trust: Notaries in Early Modern Rome*. Baltimore: Johns Hopkins University Press.

O'Malley, J. (2004). "The Society of Jesus." In R. Po-chia Hsia, ed., *A Companion to the Reformation World*. Oxford: Blackwell, pp. 223–236.

Palmieri, P. (2018). "Interactions between Orality, Manuscript and Print Culture in Sixteenth-Century Italy: Recent Historiographical Trends." *Storia Della Storiografia*, 73, No. 1: 135–148.

Paret, P. (1997). *Imagined Battles*. Chapel Hill: University of North Carolina Press.

Park, K. and L. Daston (1998). *Wonders and the Order of Nature, 1150–1750*. New York: Zone Books.

Parker, G. (1973). "Mutiny and Discontent in the Spanish Army of Flanders 1572–1607." *Past & Present*, 58: 38–52.

Parker, G. (1996 [2]). *The Military Revolution. Military Innovation and the Rise of the West, 1500–1800*. Cambridge: Cambridge University Press.

Parker, G. (2007). "The Limits to Revolutions in Military Affairs: Maurice of Nassau, the Battle of Nieuwpoort (1600), and the Legacy." *The Journal of Military History*, 71, No. 2: 331–372.

Parker, G. (2014). *Imprudent King: A New Biography of Philip II*. New Haven: Yale University Press.

Petitjean, J. (2013). *L'Intelligence des choses: une histoire de l'information entre Italia et Méditerranée (XVI–XVII siècles)*. Rome: École française de Rome.

Pettegree, A. (2005). *Reformation and the Culture of Persuasion*. Cambridge: Cambridge University Press.

Pettegree, A. (2010). *The Book in the Renaissance*. New Haven: Yale University Press.

Pettegree, A. (2014). *The Invention of News: How the World Came to Know about Itself*. New Haven, CT: Yale University Press.

Pettegree, A. (2017). "Broadsheets. Single-sheet Publishing in the First Age of Print: Typology and Typography." In A. Pettegree, ed. *Broadsheets: Single-sheet Publishing in the First Age of Print*. Leiden: Brill, 3–32.

Pettegree, A. and Hall, M. (2004). "The Reformation and the Book: A Reconsideration." *The Historical Journal*, 47, No. 4: 785–808.

Pieper, R. (1992). "Le corrispondenze dal nuovo mondo nel tardo xvi secolo sull'esempio delle Fuggerzeitungen." In A Prosperi and W. Reinhard, eds. *Il nuovo mondo nella coscienza italiana e tedesca del cinquecento*. Bologna: Il Mulino, 183–206.

Plebani, T. (1999). "La corrispondenza nell'antico regime." In Zarri, G., ed. *Per lettera: La scrittura epistolare femminile tra archivio e tipografia secoli XV-XVII*. Rome: Viella, 43–79.

Powell, W. S. (1952). "John Pory on the Death of Sir Walter Raleigh." *The William and Mary Quarterly*, 9, No. 4: 532–538.

Powell, W. S. (1977). *John Pory, 1572–1636: The Life and Letters of a Man of Many Parts. Microfiche Supplement, Letters and Other Minor Writings*. Chapel Hill: University of North Carolina Press.

Prosperi, A. (2025). *Cambiare la storia. Falsi, apocrifi, complotti*. Milan: Einaudi.

Ramos Pérez, D. (1983). *La carta de Colón sobre el Descubrimiento*. Granada: Diputación provincial.

Raymond, J. (2025). *The Great Exchange: Making the News in Early Modern Europe*. New York: Random House.

Raymond, J. and N. Moxham, eds. (2016). *News Networks in Early Modern Europe*. Leyden: Brill.

Richardson, B. (1999). *Printing, Writers and Readers in Renaissance Italy*. Cambridge: Cambridge University Press.

Ricoeur, P. (1984). *Time and Narrative*. Translated by K. McLaughlin and D. Pellauer. 3 vols. Chicago: University of Chicago Press.

Roper, A. (2017). "German Music Broadsheets, 1500 to 1550: Production, Persuasion and Performance." In A. Pettegree, ed. *Broadsheets: Single-Sheet Publishing in the First Age of Print*. Leiden: Brill, 401–441.

Rosa, H. (2013). *Social Acceleration: A New Theory of Modernity*. Tr. J. Trejo-Mathys. New York: Columbia University Press.

Rospocher, M. (2017). "La miscellanea del cardinale: La battaglia della Polesella tra stampa, manoscritto e oralità." In G. Ciappelli and V. Nider, eds. *La invención de las noticias: Las relaciones de sucesos entre la literatura y la información*, Collana Labirinti, 168. Trent: Università degli Studi di Trento, 31–50.

Rospocher, M. and Salzberg, R. (2021). *Il mercato dell'informazione: Notizie vere, false e sensazionali nella Venezia del Cinquecento*. Venice: Marsilio.

Rubin, J. (2014). "Printing and Protestants: An Empirical Test of the Role of Printing in the Reformation." *Review of Economics and Statistics* 96, No. 2: 270–286.

Runciman, S. (1965). *The Fall of Constantinople, 1453*. Cambridge: Cambridge University Press.

Salzberg, R. (2014). *Ephemeral City: Cheap Print and Urban Culture in Renaissance Venice*. Manchester: Manchester University Press.

Samoes, M. G. (1990). "Gli avisi dall'altro mondo: La ricezione veneziana delle lettere gesuitiche sul Brasile del secolo XVI." In A. Caracciolo Aricò, *L'impatto della scoperta dell'America nella cultura veneziana*. Rome: Bulzoni, 343–350.

Sardella, P. (1949). *Nouvelles et spéculations à Venise au début du XVIe siècle.* Paris: Librairie Armand Colin.

Schnurr, E.-M. (2009). *Religionskonflikt und Öffentlichkeit: Eine Mediengeschichte des Kölner Kriegs (1582–1590).* Cologne-Weimar-Vienna: Böhlau Verlag.

Schröder, T. (1995). *Die ersten Zeitungen: Textgestaltung und Nachrichtenauswahl.* Tübingen: Narr.

Schroeder, H. J. (1937). *Disciplinary Decrees of the General Councils, Text, Translation, and Commentary.* London: Herder.

Schulz, W. (1976). *Die Konstruktion von Realität in den Nachrichtenmedien.* Freiburg/ Munich: Verlag Karl Alber.

Sicilia Cardona, E. F. (2013). *La Batalla de Nieuport 1600. Los Tercios de Flandes en la "Batalla de las dunas."* Madrid: Almena.

Thomas, W. (2020). "How a Defeat became a Victory: The Siege of Ostend in Contemporary Dutch War Coverage and Post-war Chronicles (1601–15)." In Raymond Fagel, L. Álvarez Francés, B. Santiago Belmonte, eds. *Early Modern War Narratives.* Manchester: Manchester University Press, 125–45.

Varlik, N. (2015). *Plague and Empire in the Early Modern Mediterranean World: The Ottoman Experience, 1347–1600.* Cambridge: Cambridge University Press.

Vasoli, C. (1989). *Francesco Patrizi da Cherso.* Rome: Bulzoni.

Visceglia, M.A. (2015). "Politica internazionale, fazioni e partiti nella Curia Romana del tardo Cinquecento." *Rivista Storica Italiana* 127: 721–769.

Vocelka, K. (1985). *Rudolf II. und seine Zeit.* Vianna: Böhlau.

Watt, T. (1991). *Cheap Print and Popular Piety, 1550–1640.* Cambridge: Cambridge University Press.

Weber, J. (2005). "Straßburg 1605: Die Geburt der Zeitung." *Jahrbuch für Kommunikationsgeschichte* 7: 3–26.

Whipday, E. (2024). "'A True Reporte': News and the Neighbourhood in Early Modern Domestic Murder Texts." In S. F. Davies and P. Fletcher, eds. *News in Early Modern Europe: Currents and Connections.* Leiden: Brill, 159–74.

Wilkinson, A. S. (2004). *Mary Queen of Scots and French Public Opinion, 1542–1600.* Basingstoke, Hampshire: Palgrave Macmillan.

Zarri, G., ed. (1999). *Per lettera: La scrittura epistolare femminile tra archivio e tipografia, secoli XV-XVII.* Rome: Viella.

Acknowledgments

Research for this Element was conducted under grants provided by the Gladys Krieble Delmas Foundation, the National Endowment for the Humanities (USA), and the Irish Research Council Advanced Laureate scheme. The author is grateful to all of these and to the many colleagues who offered insights and criticisms to improve the content here presented. A special thanks goes to Peter Burke, Mario Infelise, Nicholas Brownlees, Mario Rizzo and John Henderson.

Cambridge Elements ≡

The Renaissance

John Henderson
Birkbeck, University of London, and Wolfson College, University of Cambridge

John Henderson is Emeritus Professor of Italian Renaissance History at Birkbeck, University of London, and Emeritus Fellow of Wolfson College, University of Cambridge. His recent publications include *Florence Under Siege: Surviving Plague in an Early Modern City* (2019), and *Plague and the City*, edited with Lukas Engelmann and Christos Lynteris (2019), and *Representing Infirmity: Diseased Bodies in Renaissance Italy*, edited with Fredrika Jacobs and Jonathan K. Nelson (2021). He is also the author of *Piety and Charity in Late Medieval Florence* (1994); *The Great Pox: The French Disease in Renaissance Europe*, with Jon Arrizabalaga and Roger French (1997); and *The Renaissance Hospital: Healing the Body and Healing the Soul* (2006). Forthcoming publications include a Cambridge Element, *Representing and Experiencing the Great Pox in Renaissance Italy* (2023).

Jonathan K. Nelson
Syracuse University Florence

Jonathan K. Nelson teaches Italian Renaissance Art at Syracuse University Florence and is research associate at the Harvard Kennedy School. His books include *Filippino Lippi* (2004, with Patrizia Zambrano); *Leonardo e la reinvenzione della figura femminile* (2007), *The Patron's Payoff: Conspicuous Commissions in Italian Renaissance Art* (2008, with Richard J. Zeckhauser), *Filippino Lippi* (2022); and he co-edited *Representing Infirmity. Diseased Bodies in Renaissance Italy* (2021). He co-curated museum exhibitions dedicated to Michelangelo (2002), Botticelli and Filippino (2004), Robert Mapplethorpe (2009), and Marcello Guasti (2019), and two online exhibitions about Bernard Berenson (2012, 2015). Forthcoming publications include a Cambridge Element, *Risks in Renaissance Art: Production, Purchase, Reception* (2023).

Assistant Editor
Sarah McBryde, *Birkbeck, University of London*

Editorial Board
Wendy Heller, *Scheide Professor of Music History, Princeton University*
Giorgio Riello, *Chair of Early Modern Global History, European University Institute, Florence*
Ulinka Rublack, *Professor of Early Modern History, St Johns College, University of Cambridge*
Jane Tylus, *Andrew Downey Orrick Professor of Italian and Professor of Comparative Literature, Yale University*

About the Series
Timely, concise, and authoritative, Elements in the Renaissance showcases cutting-edge scholarship by both new and established academics. Designed to introduce students, researchers, and general readers to key questions in current research, the volumes take multi-disciplinary and transnational approaches to explore the conceptual, material, and cultural frameworks that structured Renaissance experience.

Cambridge Elements

The Renaissance

Elements in the Series

Cinderella's Glass Slipper: Towards a Cultural History of Renaissance Materialities
Genevieve Warwick

The Renaissance on the Road: Mobility, Migration and Cultural Exchange
Rosa Salzberg

Measuring in the Renaissance: An Introduction
Emanuele Lugli

Elite Women and the Italian Wars, 1494–1559
Susan Broomhall and Carolyn James

Risks in Renaissance Art: Production, Purchase, and Reception
Jonathan K. Nelson and Richard J. Zeckhauser

Senses of Space in the Early Modern World
Nicholas Terpstra

Plague, Towns and Monarchy in Early Modern France
Neil Murphy

The French Disease in Renaissance Italy: Representation and Experience
John Henderson

The Many Lives of Täsfa Ṣeyon: An Ethiopian Intellectual in Early Modern Rome
Matteo Salvadore, James De Lorenzi, Deresse Ayenachew Woldetsadik

Who Owns Literature?: Early Modernity's Orphaned Texts
Jane Tylus

*The Fabric of War: The Material Culture and Social Lives
of Banners in Renaissance Europe*
John Gagné and Timothy McCall

Making News in Renaissance Europe
Brendan Dooley

A full series listing is available at: www.cambridge.org/EREN

For EU product safety concerns, contact us at Calle de José Abascal, 56–1°,
28003 Madrid, Spain or eugpsr@cambridge.org.

www.ingramcontent.com/pod-product-compliance
Lightning Source LLC
LaVergne TN
LVHW011852060526
838200LV00054B/4296